C000143917

How Do Vegans Get Their Protein? (B&W)

by

GEOFF AND VICKY WELLS

LIVING LIFE ON THE VEG

Learn How to Eat Great While You Lose Weight, Get Healthy and Save the Planet With an Easy Vegan Diet Plan

Copyright© 2020 by Geoff & Vicky Wells

All rights reserved

No part of this book may be used or reproduced in any manner whatsoever without prior written permission from the publisher, except for the inclusion of brief quotations in reviews.

Cover Artwork & Design by

Old Geezer Designs

Published in the United States by
Reluctant Vegetarians
an imprint of
DataIsland Software LLC,
Grand Portage, Minnesota

ISBN: 9798649643931

https://geezerguides.com

All product and company names are trademarks™ or registered® trademarks of their respective holders. Use of them does not imply any affiliation with or endorsement by them.

INTRODUCTION

This new book by The Reluctant Vegetarians, Geoff and Vicky Wells, is packed full of useful information for people who are already vegan/ vegetarian as well as for those who are interested in this healthy lifestyle.

The authors cover the important things that beginners and seasoned vegans want to know:

- What is a Vegan Diet
- Important Food Groups for a Healthy Diet
- An Overview Protein-Rich Foods
- The Best Foods for Weight Management
- The Importance of Exercise
- Common Mistakes to Avoid
- Meal Planning
- Example Recipes

EAT GREAT

Contrary to popular opinion, vegans have a wide variety of food choices at their disposal. Check out the recipes at the end of this book for just a small "taste" of the dizzying array of dishes available for breakfast, lunch, dinner, snacks and even desserts. All tasty, nutritious and easy to make.

LOSE WEIGHT

Weight loss is not the goal of this book - nutrition - and particularly getting enough protein - is what this book is about. However, when you start to eat this way, you'll find that all the nutrition, fiber, protein, etc, will, most likely, result in weight loss. Particularly if you've been eating the Standard American Diet (SAD).

SAVE THE PLANET

Yes, climate change is real. However, most people don't seem to talk about the impact that raising food animals has on our environment. If we all eat less meat - or - better still - stop eating meat all together - we can have a serious impact on lessening our carbon footprint.

Table of Contents

Lunch Recipes

Dinner Recipes

Seitan Recipes - AKA "Fake" Meat

Soups

Desserts

Condiments/Sauces

Salad Dressings

Bonus Recipes

Super Quick and Easy Meals

Bonus Recipes for the Instant Pot®

Unannounced Bonus

Other Books In The Reluctant Vegetarian Series

When someone calls themselves a vegan, that normally means that they avoid consuming or using any animal-based products.

A vegan's goal, frequently, is to attempt to eliminate the exploitation of animals, and the cruelty that entails, from anything they consume or wear.

That means they don't consume meat, poultry, fish, eggs, honey or dairy products. It also means that they refrain from wearing wool, leather or silk.

How is a Vegetarian different from a Vegan?

Vegetarians come in several different "flavors" and while a lot of the above also applies to them, some of it doesn't depending on the type of vegetarian diet they have chosen to follow.

Here's a few of the different types of vegetarians:

- **lacto** - this type of vegetarian will eat dairy
- **ovo** - this type of vegetarian will eat eggs
- **ovo-lacto** - this type of vegetarian will eat both eggs and dairy
- **pescatarian** - this type of vegetarian will eat seafood
- **pollotarian** - this is considered "semi-vegetarian" as this diet allows the consumption of poultry but generally excludes meat or seafood
- **flexitarian** - this is considered "mostly vegetarian" but they will occasionally consume meat, dairy, eggs, poultry and seafood

The interest in and acceptance of a vegan diet is a growing trend according to both **The Economist** and **Forbes** who declared 2019 "The Year of the Vegan".

https://worldin2019.economist.com/theyearofthevegan

https://www.forbes.com/sites/davidebanis/2018/12/31/everything-is-ready-to-make-2019-the-year-of-the-vegan-are-you/#7eec6e2a57df

The Growth of Veganism In the US and the World

Forbes cites a Global Data report that US consumers identifying as vegan grew from 1% of the population to 6% of the population - a 600% increase between 2014 and 2017.

https://www.forbes.com/sites/janetforgrieve/2018/11/02/picturing-a-kindler-gentler-world-vegan-month/#62b7c9602f2b

In the UK **The Vegan Society** claims that "The number of vegans in Great Britain quadrupled between 2014 and 2018."

https://www.vegansociety.com/news/media/statistics

In Canada, according to an article by **CTV News** more than 3 million Canadians now consider themselves either vegan or vegetarian.

https://www.ctvnews.ca/canada/more-than-3-million-canadians-vegetarian-or-vegan-study-1.4027606,

MAINSTREAM

It is becoming clear that veganism and vegetarianism are no longer "fringe" lifestyles nor cults or religious doctrine, as some had believed.

According to Wikipedia https://en.wikipedia.org/wiki/Veganism, "The vegan diet became increasingly mainstream in the 2010s, especially in the latter half."

REASONS WHY PEOPLE ARE BECOMING VEGANS

Reasons can include some, or all, of the following:

- to get healthier
- to lose weight
- to stop the overuse of antibiotics in meat animals
- to eliminate cruelty to farmed animals
- to decrease the environmental impact of raising food animals
- to reduce the risk of diseases like type 2 diabetes and cancer
- for religious reasons
- to lower food costs
- to lessen or eliminate the consumption of cholesterol

LET'S TALK ABOUT THE WORD "DIET"

Unfortunately, the word "diet" (a four-letter word, by the way) can conjure up many negative connotations for most people. It has for us, too, so you're not alone.

People hear "diet" and they think; starvation, deprivation, regimentation, elimination of all your favorite foods and more … You see, most people equate "diet" with a temporary method, a temporary inconvenience that they have to suffer through in order to lose some weight.

If you're like us, you've already learned that diets don't work. Oh sure, you'll lose some weight if you stick to it for a while, but if you haven't changed your lifestyle, once you've achieved your weight loss, you'll slide back into your old habits and gain all the weight back that you worked so hard to lose. Not only that, frequently you'll gain back MORE weight than you lost. It's depressing, we know.

When we refer to "diet" in this book, we're referring to a lifestyle and a way of eating that is adopted for life because it promotes health and wellbeing. While weight loss may be a result of this lifestyle, it is not the primary goal.

BENEFITS

When done correctly, a vegan or vegetarian diet, based largely on plant-based whole foods, can lead to many health benefits, such as weight loss, improved blood glucose control, disease prevention and more.

WHY WE WROTE THIS BOOK

The aim of this book is to be a beginner's guide to a vegan diet that ensures sufficient consumption of protein. It supplies information, not only about following a vegan diet, but also contains information about vegan sources of proteins, vitamins, minerals, nutrients and micronutrients.

Vegans, and often vegetarians, too, consume plant-based foods such as:

- grains
- legumes
- fruits
- vegetables
- nuts
- seeds

While that seems like a rather short list, we actually have a vast array of foods to choose from and we'll go into that later in the book.

More and more people are choosing a vegan diet for a multitude of reasons. It helps that it is now considered not only acceptable, but mainstream. Vegans are no longer decried as "fringe", "out there", "delusional" or (our favorite) "woo-woo."

Each person's motives for making the switch can encompass many things:

- personal ethics
- ecological/environmental issues
- a desire for health and wellbeing

BUT WHAT ABOUT …

We've all heard the remarks like; "But where do you get your protein?", "That can't possibly be healthy.", "What about calcium?"

Sometimes the questions seem endless. And, sometimes, they are said with a level of animosity from people who, for some reason, seem to think a vegan lifestyle threatens them in some way. We're still trying to figure that out. But, mostly, they are either genuinely concerned or are anxious to learn. So be patient with them.

Contrary to some popular beliefs, vegans don't just eat salads. As a matter of fact, since becoming vegan, we find that our choices have exploded and we're learning more each day about how to make tasty and interesting meals.

To be honest, when we were meat-eaters/omnivores, our choices were pretty boring. Each meal consisted of a meat, a vegetable (one that went with whatever meat we chose) and a starch (usually potato or rice). Each day was a slight variation of this combination. Sure, there were roasts, stews, ribs, etc. but it still amounted to the same thing - meat - veggie - starch.

But, if you're looking for something familiar as you adopt this new lifestyle, it's easy to make a lot of your favorite dishes vegan.

Here's a few ideas (and look for recipes at the end of the book):

- pasta dishes (Italian and otherwise)
- Chinese stir fries
- Indian curries
- Thai dishes
- "meat" loaf made with beans, lentils, etc.
- veggie burgers
- veggie sausages
- hot dogs made with carrots - that's right, carrots!
- granola
- "nice" cream - made with frozen bananas
- non-dairy milks and cheeses
- meat substitutes made with seitan
- breads
- cakes
- pies
- muffins

The possibilities are almost endless ...

Vegans avoid consuming any animal flesh, animal byproducts or meals containing a component from an animal source.

These include:

- meat and poultry: Steak, lamb, pork, veal, organ meat, wild game, poultry, turkey, goose, duck, quail, etc.
- seafood: all kinds of fish, anchovies, shrimp, squid, scallops, calamari, mussels, crab, lobster, etc.
- dairy: milk, yogurt, cheese, butter, cream, ice cream, etc.
- eggs: from chickens, quails, ostriches, fish, etc.
- bee products: honey, bee pollen, royal jelly, etc.
- animal-based ingredients such as whey, casein, lactose, egg white albumen, gelatin, cochineal or carmine, isinglass, shellac, L-cysteine, animal-derived vitamin D3 and fish-derived omega-3 fatty acids

TYPES OF VEGAN DIETS

As the idea of being vegan expands and includes more and more people, a few types of vegan diets have emerged. This isn't to say we need to follow any specific "diet." We only need to be cognizant of what we eat and why.

Here's a few variations that seem to be the most popular:

WHOLE-FOOD

This type strives to keep as close to the "whole" food as possible. It can also be referred to as WFPB (Whole Food Plant-Based). It includes a wide selection of complete plant foods like fruits, veggies, whole grains, legumes, nuts, and seeds. Frequently, followers of this plan also avoid any type of oil.

RAW-FOOD

This diet promotes uncooked fruits, veggies, seeds, nuts, or plant foods cooked in temperatures under 118°F (48°C). This is because nutrients can be lost when certain foods are heated above this temperature.

The 80/10/10 vegan diet is a raw-food vegan diet that restricts fat-rich plants like avocados and nuts and is based chiefly on fruits and tender greens instead. This is also known as the minimal fat, raw-food vegetarian diet, or fruitarian diet.

THE STARCH OPTION

The starch solution is a very low fat, high-carb diet much like this 80/10/10 but that concentrates on cooked starches such as potatoes, rice and corn rather than fruit.

JUNK-FOOD VEGAN DIET

This designation is just to highlight the fact that, while many processed foods can be considered vegan, that doesn't mean they are good for you. This type of vegan diet, based mostly on processed foods, fried foods and vegan desserts, is definitely NOT recommended.

Although several variations of the vegan diet exist, it's best to use common sense and stick to foods that are closest to their original form when possible. Any processed or packaged foods should be a rare indulgence.

HEALTH ADVANTAGES OF A VEGAN DIET

There are many health advantages to adopting a vegan diet. Here's just a few of them.

CARDIO VASCULAR HEALTH

A vegan diet may help to keep your heart healthy. Observational research finds that vegans may have up to a 75 percent lower chance of developing high blood pressure along with a 42 percent lower risk of dying from cardiovascular disease.

Several reports state that vegan diets are far more capable of reducing blood glucose, LDL and total cholesterol compared to standard North American diets. These effects may be especially beneficial because lowering blood pressure, cholesterol and blood glucose may decrease cardiovascular disease risk by up to 46 percent.

WEIGHT LOSS

When compared to meat-eaters, vegans often have a reduced body mass index (BMI). Vegan diets aid in reducing calories and increasing fiber, leading to weight loss.

BLOOD SUGAR AND TYPE 2 DIABETES

Many studies show that vegans have reduced glucose levels and greater insulin sensitivity. This gives them a more than 70 percent lower chance of developing type 2 diabetes.

REDUCED CANCER RISK

Vegans may benefit from a 15 percent lower risk of developing or dying from cancer.

REDUCED RISK OF ARTHRITIS

Vegan diets appear to be especially good at reducing symptoms of arthritis like pain, joint swelling and morning stiffness by reducing overall inflammation.

IMPROVED KIDNEY FUNCTION

Individuals with diabetes, who replace meat with plant-based protein, can decrease their risk of impaired kidney function.

REDUCED RISK OF ALZHEIMER'S DISEASE

Observational research demonstrates that aspects of a vegan diet can reduce the risk of developing Alzheimer's disease.

CAVEAT

Keep in mind that the majority of these studies are observational. This makes it difficult to ascertain if a vegan diet immediately caused the positive aspects. Randomized, controlled studies are required before definitive conclusions can be drawn.

IMPORTANT FOOD GROUPS FOR A HEALTHY VEGAN DIET

*I*n order to eliminate all kinds of animal exploitation and cruelty, vegans avoid conventional sources of iron and protein like poultry, meat, eggs and fish. Therefore, vegans need to include protein and iron-rich plant-based sources in their diets from foods like legumes, nuts, seeds, whole grains, fruits and seaweed.

Below is a list of food groups that will help you achieve balanced nutrition on a vegan diet:

LEGUMES

Legumes are excellent sources of:

- protein
- fiber
- slowly digested carbohydrates
- iron
- folate
- manganese
- zinc
- antioxidants
- and other health-promoting plant compounds

We need to be aware that some legumes like beans, peas and lentils can also include some anti-nutrients, which can lower the absorption of nutritional supplements. It is a good idea to sprout, ferment or cook beans well as this will reduce the effect of anti-nutrients. Try to avoid having them together with calcium-rich foods.

However, eating beans together with vitamin C rich fruits and vegetables will help improve the absorption of iron.

NUTS AND SEEDS

Nuts, seeds and butter made from either nuts or seeds, are healthy, versatile foods rich in protein and nutrients. Many vegans include them in their diets. A one ounce (28-gram) serving of nuts or seeds contains 5-12 grams of protein.

Nuts and seeds are also great sources of iron, magnesium, fiber, zinc, selenium and vitamin E, as well as antioxidants and other beneficial plant chemicals.

WHOLE GRAINS, CEREALS AND PSEUDO CEREALS

Whole grains, cereals and pseudo cereals are all good sources of complex carbohydrates, fiber and iron, in addition to B vitamins, magnesium, phosphorus and selenium.

Some forms are more nutritious than others, particularly when it comes to protein. Ancient grains spelt and teff have 10-11 grams of protein per cooked cup (237 ml). That is a lot compared to rice and wheat.

Pseudo cereals, like amaranth and quinoa, come in a close second with approximately 9 grams of protein per cooked cup (237 ml).

FRUITS AND BERRIES

Fruits, and especially berries, pack an amazing antioxidant punch. Always be sure to include fruits and berries daily.

There are lots of ways to use them from raw to cooked and even frozen.

Here's a few examples of how to include fruits and berries in your diet:

- applesauce (unsweetened, of course) is a great substitute for oil in baking
- mashed bananas can be substituted for eggs in baking
- berries of all sorts can be eaten raw or included in muffins, oatmeal, smoothies and more
- frozen bananas can be used to make "nice" cream, a non-dairy ice cream (https://blog.reluctantvegetarians.com/pina-colada-nice-cream-dessert/)

SEAWEED

While we, personally, don't tend to include seaweed in our regular diet, a lot of vegans do, so we thought it was important to mention it.

Seaweed is a protein-rich supply of essential fatty acids. It's also full of antioxidants and potassium.

Algae, like spirulina and chlorella, are also great sources of protein, two tablespoons (30 ml) supplies about 8 grams of protein. Additionally, seaweed contains magnesium, riboflavin, manganese, potassium, iodine and antioxidants.

It's important to notice that some sorts of seaweed (like kelp) are exceptionally high in acid, and need to be consumed in moderate quantities.

IMPORTANT NUTRIENTS FOR VEGANS

It's important for vegans to be aware of the nutrients in their diet so they can be sure to get adequate amounts.

GETTING ENOUGH CALCIUM

Even though drinking cow's milk for calcium is a fallacy, we still need to be sure we're getting enough absorbable calcium in our diet.

While calcium-fortified, plant-based milks and yogurts can certainly help, there are also many other plant-based foods that contain calcium.

Here's a list of the top five easily found, calcium-rich, plant-base foods (bok choy and almonds tied for first place):

- bok choy
- almonds
- spinach
- kale
- broccoli
- cabbage

Also see

https://reluctantvegetarians.com/top-5-common-calcium-rich-plant-based-foods/

GETTING ENOUGH PROTEIN

As vegans we often hear, "Where do you get your protein?", and you will too if you decide to adopt a vegan or vegetarian lifestyle.

Most meat-eaters don't seem to realize that most of the meats they eat come from herbivores - plant eaters. Yet, those meat animals grow big and strong. So, where do the animals get their protein? From plants, of course!

Here's a list of the top five common, protein-rich, plant-based foods:

- lentils
- nuts and seeds
- beans
- green peas
- rolled oats
- broccoli (honorable mention - it's actually 6th)

Also see

https://reluctantvegetarians.com/top-5-common-protein-rich-plant-based-foods/

VITAMIN B12

Vitamin B12 is of particular concern to vegans but don't be obsessed with it. Non-vegans can derive this vitamin from eating meat. Generally, most vegans are not usually B12 deficient. If you're concerned, ask your doctor to be tested.

We use fortified nutritional yeast, from time to time, as our source of B12. Nutritional yeast is created from a deactivated breed of Saccharomyces cerevisiae yeast.

It can be found, in powder or flake form, in some supermarkets, bulk foods stores and health food shops.

One ounce (28 g) contains approximately 14 grams of protein and 7 grams of fiber. Additionally, nutritional yeast is often fortified with magnesium, manganese and B vitamins, including vitamin B12, making fortified nutritional yeast a protein-rich supply of vitamin B12.

Geoff insists we mention Marmite™ as a perfect vegetarian source of, not only B12, but also Thiamin, Riboflavin, Niacin and Iron.

SPROUTED AND FERMENTED FOODS

Both sprouting and fermenting are time-tested and simple ways to increase the amount of beneficial nutrients in plant-based foods.

Sprouting can also marginally reduce the amount of gluten found in certain grains.

Fermented foods are great sources of probiotic bacteria, which could help improve immune system function and digestive health.

You can try sprouting or fermenting in your own home. A quick Google search will present you with instructions and options.

Many sprouted and fermented foods such as Ezekiel bread, tempeh, miso, sauerkraut, pickles, kimchee and kombucha can be purchased in supermarkets and specialty shops.

Sprouting and fermenting foods helps improve their nutritional value. Fermented foods also offer a supply of probiotics and vitamin K2.

CHOLINE-RICH FOODS

Choline is essential for liver, brain and nervous system health. Choline can be found, in small quantities, in a large array of fruits, vegetables, legumes, nuts, and grains. However, the plant-based foods with the most significant amounts include tofu, soy milk, broccoli, cauliflower and quinoa.

Daily choline requirements increase during pregnancy. Endurance athletes, heavy drinkers and postmenopausal women may also be at a greater risk of deficiency and should choose choline-rich foods.

OTHER CONSIDERATIONS

There are always other things to consider when adapting to a vegan diet. Here's a couple more things to think about.

CRAVING THE MEAT MOUTH-FEEL?

Eggplant, jackfruit and mushrooms (particularly Cremini or Portobello) are a good way to add a meaty texture to your meal. Try them in casseroles, stir-fries, barbecue dishes, as pizza toppings and more.

SHOULD YOU CONSIDER SUPPLEMENTS?

A well planned plant-based diet can help vegans remain healthy and prevent nutrient deficiencies. However, if you feel you're not getting enough of the nutrients you need, check with your doctor about adding supplements to your diet.

Personally, we don't take any supplements at all.

OVERVIEW OF A PROTEIN-RICH VEGAN DIET

Most non-vegans don't realize that plants contain protein. When we consume meat, that meat has protein because the meat animal (cows, pigs, chickens, etc.) eat plants. We never seem to question where herbivorous animals get their protein. It's kind of a disconnect.

So, if we're eating a balanced vegan diet, we really don't need to worry if we're getting enough protein. However, let's take a look at the numerous ways we can include protein in our vegan diet.

The first step is to be aware of the high-protein plant-based foods that are available. This way, we'll be able to make informed choices for our meal plans.

To get you started, here's a list of some high protein, plant-based choices:

- quinoa
- tofu
- tempeh
- edamame
- lentils
- chickpeas (aka garbanzo beans)
- almonds
- hemp seeds
- broccoli
- bok choy
- pumpkin seeds
- and more …

HOW MUCH PROTEIN DO WE ACTUALLY NEED?

The recommended daily allowance (RDA), established by the National Academy of Medicine, is 46 grams per day for women and 56 grams per day for men. Looking at the list of high-protein, plant-based foods, these targets are easy to reach.

Some people will need more protein than the RDA because of their daily activities. For example, weightlifters, bodybuilders and very physically active people often need more protein to support muscle repair and growth. These people should aim for 1.2 to 1.8 grams of protein per kilogram of body weight each day, according to Chris Mohr, Ph.D., RD.

For a person who weighs 160 pounds, that would be 87 to 130 grams per day.

ARE PLANT PROTEINS COMPLETE?

Most people mistakenly assume that plant protein is of lesser value than animal protein.

A widespread myth is that, in order to get sufficient amino acids, you have to eat "complementary" plant proteins together at each meal. Complementary protein foods are thought to be those that add any low or missing amino acids of the other protein source.

Here's what you need to know. Incomplete proteins—like whole grains, nuts and produce—can join together and produce a complete protein, packed with all nine essential amino acids that the body cannot produce on its own.

As long as you consume foods from various sources throughout the day, you'll get all the amino acids you need.

However, there are some exceptions to the rule. There are some plant-based foods that provide complete proteins including soy, hemp and buckwheat.

DO WE NEED PROTEIN SUPPLEMENTS ON A VEGAN DIET?

Most vegans can get all the protein they need and then some, without needing a protein supplement.

If you feel, some days, that you have fallen short of your protein goals, you can always add a scoop of protein powder to your dessert smoothie.

You can also add some protein powder to a breakfast smoothie, along with some frozen fruit, a handful of spinach and a plant-based milk. That starts your day off with a high protein vegan meal.

Be sure to choose a high quality protein powder that's sugar free. Check the ingredients for hemp, pumpkin, sprouted rice, spirulina, peas and chia. Not only will this add protein to your smoothie, but it also adds a range of vitamins, minerals and antioxidants.

HIGH PROTEIN PLANT-BASED FOODS

*T*here are actually lots of ways for vegans to get sufficient protein in their diet. Let's take a look at some of the best ways.

SOY PRODUCTS LIKE TOFU, TEMPEH AND EDAMAME BEANS

We, personally, tend to shy away from adding soy to our diet because, sadly, most soy grown today is GMO (genetically modified organism) and we avoid GMOs. If you choose to use soy products, be sure they are organic and non-GMO.

That being said, soy products are a good source of protein:

- Firm tofu (soya bean Curds) supplies about 10 grams of protein per ½ cup
- Edamame beans (immature Soya beans) supply 8.5 grams of protein per ½ cup
- Tempeh supplies about 15 grams of protein per ½ cup

Tofu is frequently used as a meat replacement in soups or sandwiches and chicken dishes.

Soy products also include good levels of iron and calcium, making them good substitutes for dairy products

LENTILS

We find lentils are extremely versatile and use them in a lot of our favorite recipes including no-meat loafs, pasta sauces, veggie burgers and more.

Red, green or brown lentils contain lots of fiber, protein and essential nutrients, such as potassium and iron.

Cooked lentils supply 8.84 grams of protein per ½ cup

CHICKPEAS (AKA GARBANZO BEANS)

We always have lots of chickpeas around and often cook a large batch and freeze them in usable sizes, like 1½ to 2 cups, to use for hummus (great for dipping or using as a replacement for butter on a sandwich or baked potato), chickpea "no-egg" salad (see recipe at the end of the book) and for putting on our salads, too.

Cooked chickpeas are high in protein, supplying about 7.25 grams per ½ cup.

They can be eaten cold or hot, making them exceptionally versatile for lots of recipes.

PEANUTS

Peanuts are another staple in our home. We like to have them for snacks as well as using them in various recipes.

They are actually a legume, not a nut, and are rich in protein and healthy fats.

A ½ cup serving contains about 20.5 grams of protein. Peanut butter contains about 8 grams of protein per tablespoon.

Try spreading peanut butter (just ground up peanuts, not the kind containing sugar and low-quality oil) on celery. It makes a delicious, healthy, crunchy snack.

ALMONDS

Yes, you guessed it. Almonds are another staple in our home and we use them for many recipes including adding them to our homemade granola. (see recipe at the end of the book).

Almonds provide 16.5 grams of protein per ½ cup. They also supply an ideal amount of vitamin E, which is excellent for eyes and skin.

QUINOA

Quinoa is a versatile, complete protein grain that can be used as a side dish on it's own Cooked quinoa includes 8 grams of protein per cup. This grain is abundant in different nutrients, such as iron, magnesium, fiber and manganese. It's also highly elastic. Quinoa can fill in for pasta in soups and stews. It can be sprinkled on a salad or eaten as the primary course.

MUSHROOMS

Mushrooms are a popular meat replacement because of their texture. They also provide 2.5 grams of protein per cup along with a lot of other nutrients.

They can be very versatile and we like to use them in lots of recipes. You can even grill a large Portobello mushroom and use it as a substitute for a burger, putting it on a bun and topping it with all the trimmings.

CHIA SEEDS

Chia seeds are low in calories, high in fiber and also contain heart-healthy Omega-3 fatty acids. In addition, they supply 2 grams of protein per tablespoon. They can be added to a smoothie, sprinkled on oatmeal or a salad or even soaked in a plant-based milk to make a pudding.

We frequently add them to our granola.

HEMP SEEDS

Hemp seeds are a complete protein that provide 5 grams of protein per tablespoon.

We like to add them when we're making bread or granola.

RICE AND BEANS

Eaten separately, rice and beans are, individually, incomplete protein sources. However, combine them (as we often do) and they can provide up to 7 grams of protein per cup.

POTATOES

Baked and roasted are probably our favorite ways to have potatoes and we have them frequently. A large baked Russet potato provides about 8 grams of protein. Potatoes are also high in other nutrients such as potassium and vitamin C.

Instead of using butter on your baked potato, try adding two tablespoons of hummus, which itself contains about 3 grams of protein.

PROTEIN-RICH VEGETABLES

Many dark, leafy greens contain protein along with an amazing array of vitamins, minerals and other nutrients.

They can easily be combined with other plant-based foods in stir fries, casseroles, salads and more.

A medium stalk of broccoli contains about 4 grams of protein.

Kale supplies about 2 grams of protein per cup.

Spinach supplies about 1 gram of protein per cup.

SEITAN

We like to make our own seitan using Vital Wheat Gluten mixed with a liquid (usually homemade vegetable broth) and other items such as spices and nutritional yeast. We even include jackfruit in some of our recipes.

The high gluten content, of course, means that people with celiac disease or gluten intolerance should avoid it. For many others, though, it can be a protein-rich meat replacement. When cooked with soy sauce, that is rich in the amino acid lysine, seitan becomes a complete protein source that provides 21 grams per ⅓ cup.

Be sure to check out the seitan recipes at the end of the book.

FLOURS AND THE VEGAN DIET

While we're sure you already know that white flour is not good for you, you may not know about all the different kinds of flours that are available at supermarkets, bulk food stores or specialty shops.

You also may not know that many of the flours available contain significant amounts of protein.

While that is certainly good news, you want to look for the least processed flours. You'll also need to be aware of some of the calories in these flours as some of them can get pretty high.

For us, the jury is still out on gluten. We can't help wondering if the problem is gluten intolerance or glyphosate (the pesticide sprayed on wheat) intolerance.

That being said, Vicky has noticed that since she cut way back on the amount of bread she eats (and she makes all of our bread from scratch) she no longer gets acid reflux. However, it can rear it's ugly head if she over-indulges in bread. She's found she can easily tolerate two slices a day, more than that and she may experience problems.

It's important to note that gluten is a protein.

WHOLE WHEAT FLOUR

Whole wheat flour is, or should be, exactly what it sounds like - the complete kernel of wheat, ground up. Always be sure to check the label and try to buy organic if you can.

```
CALORIES PER 100 GRAMS = 340
PROTEIN PER 100 GRAMS = 13.21 GRAMS
PERCENT OF GLUTEN - 12%-15%
FIBER PER 100 GRAMS = 13.1 GRAMS
```

RYE FLOUR

While rye flour comes in light, medium and dark, we are giving the stats on just the medium. Rye flour is generally just ground up rye kernels. It's usually coarser than whole wheat.

```
CALORIES PER 100 GRAMS = 349
PROTEIN PER 100 GRAMS = 10.88 GRAMS
PERCENT OF GLUTEN = 16%
FIBER PER 100 GRAMS = 11.8 GRAMS
```

VITAL WHEAT GLUTEN (AKA HIGH GLUTEN FLOUR)

As you can see from the stats, vital wheat gluten is very high in protein. Vegans who are not gluten intolerant frequently use vital wheat gluten to make seitan, a meat substitute.

```
CALORIES PER 100 GRAMS = 370
PROTEIN PER 100 GRAMS = 75 GRAMS
PERCENT OF GLUTEN = 75%
FIBER PER 100 GRAMS - 0.6 GRAMS
```

QUINOA FLOUR

Quinoa flour is made from ground quinoa seeds and is considered a complete protein.

Quinoa flour has a slightly salty flavor and works well as an ingredient in recipes for savory breads, pasta, waffles and cornbread.

CALORIES PER 100 GRAMS = 333
PROTEIN PER 100 GRAMS = 14.29 GRAMS
PERCENT OF GLUTEN = 0% (GLUTEN-FREE)
FIBER PER 100 GRAMS = 9.5 GRAMS

COCONUT FLOUR

Coconut flour may be used in lots of ways to incorporate more protein into your meals. You can use it in your morning oatmeal, bake with it, put it in smoothies (it'll help thicken them). This versatile flour also has anti-bacterial properties and fiber, too!

CALORIES PER 100 GRAMS = 429
PROTEIN PER 100 GRAMS = 17.14 GRAMS
PERCENT OF GLUTEN = 0% (GLUTEN-FREE)
FIBER PER 100 GRAMS = 40 GRAMS

AMARANTH FLOUR

Amaranth is both gluten-free and grain-free, giving it some digestive advantages to people with grain and/or gluten intolerance. It is actually made from amaranth seed and is a great source of protein as well as iron, B vitamins, potassium, magnesium and calcium.

Because of its slightly nutty taste, Amaranth flour is best used for baking pizza crusts, muffins and breads.

CALORIES PER 100 GRAMS = 367
PROTEIN PER 100 GRAMS = 13.33 GRAMS
PERCENT OF GLUTEN = 0% (GLUTEN-FREE)
FIBER PER 100 GRAMS = 10 GRAMS

TEFF FLOUR

Teff flour has gained much more popularity recently. This tiny seed is both protein and fiber-rich. You can use this flour for baking brownies, cakes, breads, muffins, pancakes, waffles and more.

CALORIES PER 100 GRAMS = 366

PROTEIN PER 100 GRAMS = 12.2 GRAMS

PERCENT OF GLUTEN = 0% (GLUTEN-FREE)

FIBER PER 100 GRAMS = 12.2 GRAMS

SOY FLOUR

Soy is actually a legume and is gluten-free. You can easily substitute ¼ cup of soy flour for any other flour in most baked goods.

Other ways to use soy flour is for dredging vegetables before frying or for thickening sauces.

The protein in soy is considered a complete protein containing all of the essential amino acids.

Sadly, most soy grown today is GMO. So, always check the label and get organic soy when you can.

CALORIES PER 100 GRAMS = 434

PROTEIN PER 100 GRAMS = 37.81 GRAMS

PERCENT OF GLUTEN = 0% (GLUTEN-FREE)

FIBER PER 100 GRAMS = 9.6 GRAMS

GARBANZO BEAN FLOUR (AKA CHICKPEA FLOUR, AKA GRAM FLOUR, AKA BESAN)

Garbanzo bean flour, also referred to as chickpea flour, gram flour or besan, comes from dried garbanzo beans. It is most frequently used in bread and sauce recipes.

CALORIES PER 100 GRAMS = 387

PROTEIN PER 100 GRAMS = 22.39 GRAMS

PERCENT OF GLUTEN = 0% (GLUTEN-FREE)

FIBER PER 100 GRAMS = 10.8 GRAMS

BUCKWHEAT FLOUR

Buckwheat isn't actually a "wheat" but rather a grain-like seed. It is gluten-free.

It can be used to make some baked goods and, in particular, pancakes. Who hasn't tried some buckwheat pancakes?

CALORIES PER 100 GRAMS = 335
PROTEIN PER 100 GRAMS = 12.62 GRAMS
PERCENT OF GLUTEN = 0% (GLUTEN-FREE)
FIBER PER 100 GRAMS = 10.0 GRAMS

GROUND CHIA SEEDS (AKA CHIA FLOUR, AKA CHIA MEAL)

While ground chia seeds pack quite a calorie punch, they are also very high in fiber. Keep in mind, that you generally don't need to use a lot. Chia is also an amazing source of protein.

We like to use it as a healthy, gluten-free thickener and/or egg replacement in a lot of recipes.

You can also use it to make a quick and tasty pudding - see the recipe later in this book

Chia seeds are a complete protein supplying all the essential amino acids.

CALORIES PER 100 GRAMS = 500
PROTEIN PER 100 GRAMS = 25.0 GRAMS
PERCENT OF GLUTEN = 0% (GLUTEN-FREE)
FIBER PER 100 GRAMS = 41.7 GRAMS

ADDITIONAL INFORMATION

All the statistic cited for the flours mentioned above are from the USDA Food Composition Databases - https://ndb.nal.usda.gov/

As far as we're concerned, if we are informed about the composition of the foods we choose to eat, we are then able to make better choices. Always attempt to achieve a balance between calories, protein and fiber. Gluten content is also a consideration for a lot of people.

We have attempted, in this chapter, to help make choices a little easier and a bit more transparent.

BEST VEGAN FOODS FOR WEIGHT MANAGEMENT & MUSCLE BUILDING

Protein is a vital nutrient for weight loss. It boosts our metabolism and reduces hunger. Lack of protein in our diet can lead to cravings and mindless eating.

Protein not only assists in weight loss, it also prevents muscle loss. As a vegan, it's important to be aware of the protein-rich foods that are available.

The secret to a nutritionally sound vegan diet is variety. A healthy vegan diet includes fruits, vegetables, seeds, nuts, green vegetables and legumes. A vegan diet is cholesterol free and this can help stimulate muscle development.

Vegans also, in general, adopt a healthier lifestyle that includes physical exercise. This can also help with weight loss and management.

BUT WHERE DO YOU GET YOUR PROTEIN?

People who have never tried a vegan diet are often quick to tell you that you can't get enough protein to be healthy. The truth is, not only can you get plenty of protein, you can do it without the harmful saturated fats, toxins and calories in red meat.

With nuts, beans, greens and seeds you can get more protein than you could possibly need.

Virtually all plant-based sources of nutrition contain some amount of protein. Eat well and you won't need to worry about your protein intake.

Below is a list of vegan protein foods that can help to stimulate weight loss:

CHIA SEEDS

Chia seeds are packed with omega-3 fatty acids and can help to suppress appetite by activating glucagon (https://en.wikipedia.org/wiki/Glucagon), a fat burning hormone.

> CALORIES PER 100 GRAMS = 500
> PROTEIN PER 100 GRAMS = 25.0 GRAMS
> FIBER PER 100 GRAMS = 41.7 GRAMS

ALMONDS

Almonds are rich in healthy fats that can contribute to weight loss. Having a handful of almonds, from time to time, can help curb hunger.

> CALORIES PER 100 GRAMS = 571
> PROTEIN PER 100 GRAMS = 21.43 GRAMS
> FIBER PER 100 GRAMS = 10.7 GRAMS

LENTILS

Lentils are a great source of both fiber and protein. A one cup serving (192 grams) supplies over 47 grams of protein and can help maintain lean muscle mass.

> CALORIES PER 100 GRAMS = 352
> PROTEIN PER 100 GRAMS = 24.63 GRAMS
> FIBER PER 100 GRAMS = 20.7 GRAMS

QUINOA

Quinoa is a diet-friendly food filled with hunger-fighting protein. It helps to maintain a full feeling for extended periods and, therefore, can help to prevent overeating.

> CALORIES PER 100 GRAMS = 333
> PROTEIN PER 100 GRAMS = 14.29 GRAMS
> FIBER PER 100 GRAMS = 9.5 GRAMS

BEANS

Most beans, including black beans, navy beans, garbanzo beans, pinto beans and more, are very low in fat but are packed with protein and fiber, while also being low in calories.

Note: the stats below are for black beans but most beans are similar

> CALORIES PER 100 GRAMS = 68
> PROTEIN PER 100 GRAMS = 3.85 GRAMS
> FIBER PER 100 GRAMS = 5.4 GRAMS

BROCCOLI

The high fiber and water content in broccoli adds volume to meals without adding any empty calories. It's actually one of our favorite vegetables.

> CALORIES PER 100 GRAMS = 34
> PROTEIN PER 100 GRAMS = 2.82 GRAMS
> FIBER PER 100 GRAMS = 2.6 GRAMS

SPINACH

Spinach helps retain vitamins, facilitates calcium absorption and wards off bloating. It can be used raw, steamed, boiled or sautéed. We like to add it to curries, soups, salads and stews.

> CALORIES PER 100 GRAMS = 23
> PROTEIN PER 100 GRAMS = 2.86 GRAMS
> FIBER PER 100 GRAMS = 2.2 GRAMS

CHICKPEAS (AKA GARBANZO BEANS, AKA CHANA)

Chickpeas, actually a legume, provide lots of protein and fiber. Although higher in calories than a lot of beans, the fiber helps to control the calories.

> CALORIES PER 100 GRAMS = 360
> PROTEIN PER 100 GRAMS = 20.0 GRAMS
> FIBER PER 100 GRAMS = 18.0 GRAMS

VEGAN DIET AND EXERCISE

There are many advantages to exercising. It helps to make your body better and stronger.

If you regularly work out, then it is vital to get enough protein in your diet - at the right times - so your body has what it needs to build muscle.

Properly fueling your body will prevent stress and anxiety, while also preventing the release of cortisol, the stress hormone that makes it difficult to lose weight.

Post-exercise snacks and meals should be designed to help you bounce back after a demanding workout.

Following are suggestions for both snacks (immediately after a workout) and meals (at least an hour after a workout).

POST-WORKOUT SNACK

Triathlete Brendan Brazier (https://en.wikipedia.org/wiki/ Brendan_Brazier), an expert on vegan nutrition, tells us that the first 45 minutes following a challenging exercise are crucial to healing.

Digestion is somewhat sluggish after a workout. Brazier recommends that your post-workout snack should include no more than 25% protein.

For vegans, this could be some fruit and a small amount of nut butter. A plain white baked potato and some steamed green beans or carrots would also do the job. Add a little salt for taste and electrolytes.

POST-WORKOUT MEAL

A post-workout meal should be at least an hour or so following your exercise. This is the best time to load up on protein.

Your body has replenished its fuel with the carbohydrates from your snack and is now prepared to rebuild.

Ennette Larson (https://www.vrg.org/nutshell/athletes.htm), a dietician with the Vegetarian Resource Group, recommends complex carbohydrates with this meal since your body requires both carbohydrates and protein to rebuild.

Options for this meal are a veggie-packed salad with a large bowl of bean soup, bean chili on a baked potato, a stir fry with loads of veggies and some rice with a plant-based protein of your choice, etc.

If you're not particularly hungry, then a smoothie may be the way to go. Include some fruit, a plant-based milk, some hemp seeds or a vegan protein powder.

The goal here is to consume a balance of carbs and protein.

If you are training particularly hard, stay with snacks that combine protein and carbohydrates every couple of hours. These snacks can consist of raw veggies with hummus or a tiny black bean burrito with broccoli and cauliflower.

The higher the quality of your snacks and meals, the quicker your recovery.

Always stick to whole, unprocessed foods like fruits and vegetables, whole grains and legumes and drink lots of water to keep hydrated.

MISTAKES TO AVOID ON A VEGAN DIET

Sometimes it can be difficult to maintain a well-balanced vegan diet that provides all the nutrients you want and need.

A balanced vegan diet offers many health benefits:

- weight loss
- better blood glucose control
- reduced risk of cardiovascular disease
- reduced risk of certain types of cancer

Here are the most frequent mistakes made and how to prevent them.

ASSUMING THAT VEGAN PRODUCTS ARE AUTOMATICALLY HEALTHIER

Unfortunately, just because a food item is labeled "vegan" does not necessarily mean it is healthier, or even healthy at all.

Whether you are vegan or not, it's always best to avoid overly processed foods, including ones that are labeled vegan. Many highly processed foods that are advertised as "vegan" are often high in added sugar and lacking in nutrition.

Yes, sugar is actually vegan. It comes from a plant, usually from sugar cane or sugar beets. But we all know that processed sugar is bad for us.

There's nothing wrong with having some of these vegan processed foods from time to time as part of a balanced diet. However, the bulk of a vegan diet should consist of nutritious, plant-based, whole foods.

IGNORING THE IMPORTANCE OF VITAMIN B12

Vitamin B12 plays several crucial functions in the human body. It is essential in the creation of red blood cells and DNA, among other functions.

Unfortunately, the main sources of vitamin B12 are found in animal products, including poultry, meat, shellfish, eggs and dairy products.

Vegans are rarely vitamin B12 deficient, however, it is something to be aware of.

We like to use nutritional yeast, fortified with B12, in a lot of our recipes as well as sprinkling it on our spaghetti as a substitute for grated cheese.

Geoff is happy to spread some Marmite™ on toast and never think about B12 deficiency.

If you're concerned about vitamin B12 deficiency, check with your doctor.

CONSUMING TOO FEW CALORIES

Vegans tend to consume fewer calories than those who include meat in their diet. This isn't necessarily a bad thing as long as we're getting sufficient nutrition. However, restricting calories too much may result in some negative side effects, such as nutritional deficiencies, exhaustion and a slower metabolic rate.

If you maintain a balanced vegan diet, consuming fewer calories can, of course, help with weight loss, if that is one of your goals. But don't sacrifice proper nutrition for unrealistic weight loss goals.

NOT DRINKING ENOUGH WATER

Drinking sufficient water is crucial for everybody, but even more so for people who consume a lot of fiber.

Vegans tend to have greater fiber consumption because fiber-rich beans, vegetables and whole grains are staples of a healthy vegan diet.

Drinking sufficient water helps to prevent digestive difficulties related to increased fiber consumption such as gas, constipation and bloating.

NOT INCLUDING WHOLE FOODS IN YOUR DIET

A vegan diet is an opportunity to boost your consumption of nutrient-dense whole foods, like fruits, vegetables and whole grains. Eating whole foods instead of processed foods can provide additional advantages too, such as an enhanced metabolism.

Any vegan diet includes mostly whole foods. They help optimize nutrient consumption and create a more balanced diet.

NOT CONSUMING SUFFICIENT PROTEIN-RICH FOODS

On a vegan diet it really isn't that difficult to get enough protein in your diet if you're eating balanced meals. However, you might want to be more aware of which vegan foods are higher in protein.

Be sure to include such sources as:

- lentils
- nuts and seeds
- beans
- green peas (including sugar snap peas and snow peas)
- rolled oats
- broccoli

Be sure to check out a short video we made about the most common and easy to find protein-rich foods.

https://reluctantvegetarians.com/top-5-common-protein-rich-plant-based-foods/

NOT GETTING ENOUGH CALCIUM

Most people seem to believe that the best way to get enough calcium is through dairy products. This is not true.

Many plant-based foods contain high levels of calcium. Calcium-rich plant-based foods include:

- spinach
- collard greens
- broccoli
- bok choy
- almonds
- figs
- oranges

We produced a short video showing the Top Five Common Calcium-Rich Plant-Based Foods.

https://reluctantvegetarians.com/top-5-common-calcium-rich-plant-based-foods/

These are foods that you can easily find in your grocery store.

IGNORING THE IMPORTANCE OF IRON

Even non-vegans sometimes have difficulty getting enough iron in their diets.

Plant sources of iron include non-heme (not from blood) iron, which your body cannot absorb as quickly.

Non-heme iron is found in various kinds of vegetables, fruits, cereals and legumes.

Vegans should strive to consume lots of great sources of iron such as:

- legumes
- fortified cereals
- seeds
- nuts
- oats
- leafy greens

A good thing to know is that pairing spicy foods with foods high in vitamin C can help to boost the absorption of non-heme iron. Keep this in mind when planning meals.

IGNORING THE IMPORTANCE OF OMEGA-3 FATTY ACIDS

To get enough omega-3 on a vegan diet, you'll want to make sure to consume some of the following:

- chia seeds
- hemp seeds
- flaxseeds
- seaweed
- walnuts
- kidney beans

You could also consider a supplement, but, as we have said before, as long as you have a balanced diet, with lots of varied foods, you should be getting what you need.

CONSUMING TOO MANY REFINED CARBS

So that you're getting enough nutrients without adding empty calories, eliminate refined carbs from your diet.

Avoid things like:

- white bread
- pastas made from white flour
- white rice

Instead, use healthier whole grains like:

- whole grain pasta
- whole grain breads
- quinoa
- oats
- brown rice
- buckwheat

Be sure to pair these whole grains with lots of whole fruits, vegetables and legumes to maintain a healthy and balanced diet.

UNDERESTIMATING THE SIGNIFICANCE OF MEAL PLANNING

The benefits of meal planning, whether you are cooking at home or eating out, shouldn't be ignored.

If you truly want to stay on track and ensure you have a balanced diet, then meal planning should be an important part of your regimen.

We find it beneficial to plan several days, or even a week, in advance. This way it helps to make grocery shopping easier and, we find, it also helps to encourage trying new recipes. We like to identify new recipes we'd like to try, make sure we shop for the right ingredients and then either make some of them ahead and freeze them, or, at the very least, prepare what ingredients we can ahead of time to make cooking quicker and easier.

We've certainly discovered a lot of tasty and interesting meals this way.

A balanced vegan diet can be healthy, nutritious and delicious.

PROTEIN-RICH VEGAN MEAL SUGGESTIONS

In this section we provide a suggested weekly, protein-rich meal plan and give you a bunch of recipes.

But, remember, the possibilities are actually endless! So, don't limit yourself to just these suggestions and recipes.

A WEEK'S WORTH OF SUGGESTED PROTEIN-RICH VEGAN MEALS

This week of suggested meals is based on the way we actually eat. Feel free to change them up to what suits your likes/dislikes/lifestyle.

It's always a great idea to make a lot of your meals ahead of time. We do that and then freeze them. It makes for quick and easy meal prep.

We made notes on the recipes to let you know which ones freeze well.

SUNDAY

Sundays tend to be "lazy" days for us. We often like to start the day with our favorite pancakes. However, we frequently have a more elaborate dinner than we would most days. That's kind of a throw back from the Sunday dinners we both were used to as kids and continued the tradition ourselves.

BREAKFAST

Our favorite pancakes!

Gluten-Free, Sugar-Free Vegan Pancakes (see recipe on page 72)

Topping Suggestions:

- fresh fruit (we like a mix of berries)
- maple syrup (the real stuff - and just a little)
- sugar-free applesauce (shake a little cinnamon on the top)

LUNCH

A Sunday lunch should be simple.

Have a tossed green salad with your favorite vegan dressing.

Don't forget to throw a few nuts and seeds (particularly pumpkin seeds) on your salad for a protein punch!

SNACK

Snacks are totally optional but sometimes you just want a "little something" to tide you over until dinner.

Here's a few snack suggestions:

- a whole fruit, like an apple, orange, banana, grapes, cherries, etc.
- a small handful of nuts or seeds (or a mix of both)
- some peanut butter-stuffed celery

This is a full dinner, complete with gravy!

Roasted Cauliflower Dinner (see recipe on page 93)

A great way to finish a Sunday dinner is with an amazing dessert.

Piña Colada Nice Cream (see recipe on page 142)

MONDAY

Mondays can be busy days for a lot of us, so lets make it a bit easier. Be sure to make the soup ahead of time.

BREAKFAST

Vicky's Favorite Granola (see recipe on page 65)

½ cup of this protein-packed granola with about ½ cup of an unsweetened, plant-based milk and you'll be ready to face the day.

LUNCH

Soup and a sandwich makes for a tasty and satisfying lunch. Make the soup ahead of time and refrigerate or freeze in serving size containers so you can just grab it and go.

Carrot & Pumpkin Soup (see recipe on page 128)

Pair this soup with a simple sandwich or wrap containing fresh veggies like tomato, spinach, lettuce, alfalfa sprouts and a little vegan mayonnaise on some multi-grain vegan bread.

SNACK

Throw an apple, orange or some grapes in your lunch bag for an afternoon snack.

DINNER

The following is quick and full of protein, pair it with some whole grain rice for a complete meal.

Black Beans and Tomatoes (see recipe on page 82)

DESSERT

One of our favorite desserts is a bowl of mixed fruits. You can, if you like, pair it with some "nice" cream. To make the "nice" cream, just combine a frozen banana (cut into chunks), about ¼ cup of a plant-based milk and ¼ teaspoon of vanilla (optional), in your food processor and process until smooth and creamy. (Hint: put the milk in first) You'll be amazed at how much it tastes like "real" ice cream.

TUESDAY

BREAKFAST

Geoff's Mum had oatmeal for breakfast almost every day - and she lived to 102!

Hot Oatmeal (see recipe on page 68)

Feel free to dress up your oatmeal with such things as:

- pumpkin seeds
- mixed berries (usually blueberries, strawberries, raspberries and blackberries)
- sliced bananas
- chopped nuts
- unsweetened applesauce
- a splash of a plant-based milk, flavored, if you like

LUNCH

For lunch today, why not try a Seitan Roast Beeph sandwich? And, no, we didn't spell Beef wrong. We chose to spell it Beeph because it is a plant-based meat AKA "fake" meat.

Be sure to make the **Seitan Roast Beeph** ahead of time. (see recipe on page 118)

Once you've made the Roast Beeph, you can slice it up and package it in serving sizes.

Create your sandwich with some whole grain bread, condiments of your choice, a slice or two of tomato and some lettuce.

SNACK

A few whole grain crackers with a little peanut butter (or other nut butter) with a small banana make a great snack.

Hint: make sure whatever nut butter you use that it's just nuts - no added sugar, preservatives, etc. Just whole, ground-up nuts.

DINNER

We have always like slow cooker meals that we can start in the morning and they're ready by suppertime. That's what's on the menu for tonight!

Black Bean Stew in a Slow Cooker (see recipe on page 104)

All this needs is some rice, pasta or potatoes and maybe a crusty, whole grain roll.

DESSERT

Make these muffins ahead of time and keep some ready in the freezer for dessert, or even a snack.

Sugar-Free, Gluten-Free, Egg-Free, Oil-Free Strawberry Muffins (see recipe on page 146)

Have a piece of fruit with your muffin, if you like.

WEDNESDAY

BREAKFAST

A smoothie is a great idea for a busy morning. Just throw everything in a blender, blend until smooth and breakfast is ready!

Hint: Prepare the ingredients for the smoothies you want to make ahead of time. Freeze them in serving-size containers. Then just add the liquid and your pre-frozen ingredients for a quick breakfast smoothie.

Vicky's Favorite Breakfast Smoothie is a great start to a busy day. (see recipe on page 74)

LUNCH

You can't go wrong with a salad for lunch. The chickpeas and walnuts in this salad provide lots of protein!

Baby Spinach Salad (see recipe on page 86)

SNACK

As always, an afternoon snack is totally optional.

Celery stuffed with nut butter or some vegan cream cheese makes a nice, protein-packed snack.

DINNER

When we were meat-eaters, we always enjoyed a nice meat loaf for dinner. This recipe is Geoff's favorite and he says he likes it better than the "real" meatloaf we used to make.

Geoff's Favorite No-Meat Loaf (see recipe on page 96)

To complete the meal, just add potatoes done anyway you like and some veggies.

This is another dessert you can make ahead and freeze. We suggest that you slice it before you freeze it and just defrost as much as you need each time.

Banana Cake (see recipe on page 148)

THURSDAY

BREAKFAST

Let's do oatmeal again this morning! We like to have hot oatmeal at least a couple of times a week.

Here's a quick repeat of Tuesday's breakfast:

Hot Oatmeal (see recipe on page 68)

Feel free to dress up your oatmeal with such things as:

- pumpkin seeds
- mixed berries (usually blueberries, strawberries, raspberries and blackberries)
- sliced bananas
- chopped nuts
- unsweetened applesauce
- a splash of a plant-based milk, flavored, if you like

LUNCH

Make these classic baked beans ahead of time and package them up in serving sizes to make grabbing a lunch to take to work a breeze.

Basic Baked Beans in a Slow Cooker (see recipe on page 84)

SNACK

Raw veggies and hummus make a great snack. Check the recipes section for a couple of tasty hummus recipes.

DINNER

You'll find the recipe for the suggested dinner in the Bonus Recipes 2 - Recipes for the Instant Pot section of this book. Don't have an Instant

Pot®? Not to worry, just select a different dinner recipe from the recipes section - or create a new recipe of your own!

Eggplant and Sweet Potato Curry (see recipe on page 171)

DESSERT

Let's take it easy for dessert tonight and have some plain fruit.

Here's a few suggestions:

- banana slices
- apple slices
- grapes
- orange segments
- pear slices
- peach slices
- frozen mixed berries

Plan ahead and mix all the ingredients above into a delicious fresh fruit salad. Let it sit in the refrigerator overnight so all the flavors can combine.

FRIDAY

*I*t's Friday! Time to wind down and welcome the weekend.

We don't know about you, but we like Friday meals to be easy without sacrificing taste. So, here's our suggestions to do just that.

BREAKFAST

Time for another of our favorite smoothies for a quick and easy breakfast on the last work day of the week.

Very Berry Smoothie (see recipe on page 76)

LUNCH

As with all our soups, we suggest you make them ahead and package them in serving sizes. This also gives the flavors a chance to meld and makes for a tastier soup.

Easy Instant Pot® Minestrone Soup (see recipe on page 185)

SNACK

Always remember - snacks are optional. We're just giving you a few suggestions in case you need a little bit extra to tide you over until dinner.

So, today, let's just have a few nuts, seeds and maybe some raisins, too.

We like to combine:

- almonds
- peanuts
- pumpkin seeds
- sunflower seeds
- raisins

Be sure to keep the serving size very small as these are all quite high in calories but also have lots of protein and some healthy fats.

A few examples of snack sizes

DINNER

In keeping with the "keep Friday easy" theme, this dinner is both quick and tasty.

Veggie Sausages baked in Sauerkraut (see recipe on page 165)

To round out this meal add a baked potato and some steamed veggies of your choice.

DESSERT

Who says smoothies can't be desserts? Well, this one certainly can. It even has a optional "kick" to it with the addition of some rum, if desired.

Tropical Dream Smoothie (see recipe on page 144)

SATURDAY

BREAKFAST

If your Saturday isn't too hurried, you might want to try these breakfast sausage patties with some fried tomato slices and mushrooms on the side.

Breakfast "Sausage" Patties (see recipe on page 70)

LUNCH

We like to make this bean salad either a day ahead, or in the morning, to give it time to marinate a bit.

Serve it on a bed of leafy greens accompanied by a nice, crusty, whole grain bread.

Mexican Style Bean Salad (see recipe on page 88)

SNACK

A simple snack is often the best kind. This may seem a little "dull", but we like it from time to time and it's very low in calories.

Just have a few dill pickles - baby dills, dill chips, regular dills. Just enough to stave off those mid-day grumblings.

Like we said - simple.

DINNER

You won't even miss the chicken! We love this pot pie and like to serve it with mashed potatoes, steamed veggies and, yes, even cranberry sauce!

Chickpea Pot Pie (see recipe on page 98)

These muffins can be a dessert, a breakfast or a snack. On top of that, they tick all the boxes by eliminating sugar, gluten, eggs and oil! No small feat for a tasty muffin.

Sugar-Free, Gluten-Free, Egg-Free, Oil-Free Strawberry Muffins (see recipe on page 146)

EASY, HIGH-PROTEIN VEGAN RECIPES

As many of us transition to a plant-based lifestyle, we tend to worry about whether or not we're getting enough protein. That worry is usually reinforced by well-meaning omnivores (people who include meat, fish and dairy in their diets). We've all encountered it - when you tell someone you're vegan, the first question is usually, "But, where do you get your protein?"

So, we've included the amount of protein per serving with each of these recipes.

You're going to be pleasantly surprised at just how easy it is to get protein in your diet without animal products.

BREAKFAST RECIPES

A good breakfast always helps to start your day off right.

Vicky's Favorite Granola

$\mathcal{T}$his is a staple in our household and we almost go into panic mode when we run out.

Yes, it is high calorie, but it's good for us. A serving of ½ cup, with a little non-dairy milk (almond milk, coconut milk, soy milk - all non-GMO, of course), is all that you need.

INGREDIENTS

4 cups (320g) rolled oats, old fashioned, not quick or minute

½ cup (86g) chia seeds

½ cup (47g) oat bran

½ cup (74g) ground flax seed

½ cup (66g) sunflower seeds

½ cup (55g) almonds, chopped

½ cup (65g) walnuts, chopped

½ teaspoon (2.5 ml) sea salt

½ cup (90g) brown sugar

½ cup (120 ml) maple syrup

⅓ cup (80 ml) coconut oil

2 teaspoons (10 ml) ground cinnamon

1½ teaspoons (7.5 ml) vanilla extract

1 cup (150g) raisins

6 Medjool dates, pitted and chopped

1 tablespoon (15 ml) finely ground almonds

DIRECTIONS

Pre-heat the oven to 325°F (170°C, Gas Mark 3) and lightly grease a large baking sheet. Alternately, you can line the baking sheet with parchment paper. That's what we usually do because it makes for much easier clean up and nothing sticks.

Combine the oats, chia seeds, ground flax seeds, oat bran, sunflower seeds, almonds and walnuts in a large bowl.

In a small saucepan, mix together the salt, brown sugar, maple syrup, coconut oil, cinnamon and vanilla. Over medium heat, bring the mixture to a boil and immediately remove from heat.

Pour the liquid mixture over the oat mixture and stir well to coat everything evenly. Then spread the mixture evenly on the prepared baking sheet.

Bake at 325°F (170°C, Gas Mark 3) for 20 minutes. Remove from the oven and allow to cool.

While the granola is baking, chop up the Medjool dates and then toss them in the ground almonds to prevent them from sticking together.

Once the oatmeal mixture has cooled, break it up and add the raisins and dates. Toss together to mix well.

Store the completed granola in an airtight container.

Note: We wish we could tell you how long it keeps in an airtight container, but it never lasts very long in our house.

SERVINGS: 16 (BASED ON A ½ CUP SERVING)

CALORIES PER SERVING: 371 (NOT INCLUDING WHATEVER PLANT MILK YOU CHOOSE)

PROTEIN PER SERVING: 8.28 GRAMS (NOT INCLUDING WHATEVER PLANT MILK YOU CHOOSE)

Hot Oatmeal

While this may seem like a pretty boring breakfast, it's really good for you. And, you can always dress it up with healthy toppings of your choice.

Here's a few of our favorite toppings:

- pumpkin seeds
- mixed berries (usually a frozen mix of blueberries, strawberries, raspberries and blackberries)
- sliced bananas
- chopped nuts

INGREDIENTS

1 cup (80g) old fashioned rolled oats

2 cups (475 ml) water (you can replace some of the water with a plant milk of your choice)

pinch of salt

DIRECTIONS

Combine the oats and water (or water and milk) in a medium saucepan.

Bring the mixture to a boil over medium-high heat.

Reduce heat and continue cooking until nicely thickened - about 5 minutes.

Serve immediately with topping(s) of your choice.

SERVINGS: 2-3

CALORIES PER SERVING: 148 (BASED ON 2 SERVINGS/RECIPE MADE WITH WATER)

PROTEIN PER SERVING: 5.48 GRAMS (BASED ON 2 SERVINGS/ RECIPE MADE WITH WATER)

Breakfast "Sausage" Patties

*T*hese patties can be served with fried onions and a little tomato on the side or can be served in a English muffin with condiments of your choice. Don't just limit them to breakfast, either. They also make a great lunch or dinner.

INGREDIENTS

1 cup (80g) old fashioned oats, pulsed a few times in a food processor (not too much - you don't want oat flour)

¼ cup (37g) ground flax seeds

¼ cup (43g) chia seeds

¼ cup (15g) nutritional yeast

1 tablespoon (15 ml) dehydrated onion flakes

1 tablespoon (15 ml) garlic, minced

1 tablespoon (15 ml) brown sugar

2 teaspoons (10 ml) paprika

2 teaspoons (10 ml) oregano

1 teaspoon (5 ml) black pepper, freshly ground

1 teaspoon (5 ml) sage, ground

1 teaspoon (5 ml) fennel seed

1 teaspoon (5 ml) thyme

1 teaspoon (5 ml) cumin

½ teaspoon (2.5 ml) sea salt or Himalayan pink salt

¼ teaspoon (1.25 ml) cayenne pepper, ground (or to taste)

1 pinch red pepper flakes (or to taste)

¾ cup (180 ml) vegetable broth, preferably homemade

3 tablespoons (45 ml) soy sauce, preferably low sodium

1 teaspoon (5 ml) liquid smoke

1 tablespoon (15 ml) coconut oil, for frying

DIRECTIONS

In a large bowl, combine the dry ingredients. Mix well. Set aside.

In a large measuring cup, combine the wet ingredients. Mix well.

Pour the wet ingredients into the dry ingredients. Mix until everything becomes firm and holds together.

Let the mixture rest for 10 minutes. The resting period allows the chia seeds and flax to absorb the liquid.

Preheat a skillet on medium heat and add a little coconut oil.

When the skillet is hot, form the patties.

Place the patties in the skillet and cook for 1 minute or until well browned.

Turn the patties and cook for another minute or until that side is well browned.

Serve immediately.

Freeze any leftovers.

SERVINGS: 12 PATTIES
CALORIES PER SERVING: 126/PATTY
PROTEIN PER SERVING: 5.65 GRAMS/PATTY

Gluten-Free, Sugar-Free Vegan Pancakes

We like this recipe so much, we have it memorized! It's usually our choice for a lazy Sunday morning breakfast.

You'll be surprised at how much protein this tasty breakfast has!

Top with your favorite fruit.

INGREDIENTS

1½ cups (350 ml) almond milk

1½ cups (120g) old fashioned rolled oats

2 tablespoons (30 ml) unsweetened applesauce

1 tablespoon (15 ml) chia seeds

2 teaspoons (10 ml) baking powder

1 teaspoon (5 ml) vanilla

½ teaspoon (2.5 ml) salt

Tip: You may find that you need to add more milk to the batter as it can thicken up pretty quickly. So have some extra milk on hand.

DIRECTIONS

Heat your oven to the LOWEST temperature it has. (The lowest temperature in our oven is 170°F (80°C, Gas Mark ¼.)

Place your plates in the oven to warm. You'll also be placing the first batch of pancakes in the oven to keep them warm while you cook the next batch.)

Heat a large skillet over medium/high heat. Use a non-stick skillet or spray with cooking spray.

Place all of the ingredients in a blender, milk first.

Tip: Putting the milk in first helps all the other ingredients blend together more easily without clogging or stalling the blender.

Slowly increase the blending speed to maximum until all the ingredients are well blended.

Pour about ¼ of a cup (60 ml) of batter, per pancake, into the hot skillet.

Note: We usually cook 3-4 pancakes at a time in our skillet.

Cook each side about 3-4 minutes or until nicely browned.

Keep cooked pancakes warm in the oven while the rest are cooking.

Once all the pancakes are ready, serve immediately, on the warm plates, with toppings of your choice, eg berries, applesauce, maple syrup, etc.

> SERVINGS: 2 (APPROX. 4 PANCAKES PER SERVING)
> CALORIES PER SERVING: 514
> PROTEIN PER SERVING: 20.54 GRAMS

Note: check out our video for this recipe - https://blog.reluctantvegetarians.com/gluten-free-sugar-free-vegan-pancakes/

Vicky's Favorite Breakfast Smoothie

If you're using just a regular blender (we use a VitaMix) you'll need to cut things up fairly small. For a commercial grade blender, large-size chunks are fine.

INGREDIENTS

- 1 cup (240 ml) almond milk
- 1½ cups (350 ml) water
- ½ large cucumber
- 2 large carrots, peeled
- 1 medium apple, cored and sliced
- 1 small banana, frozen

1 medium pear, cored and sliced

½ inch (1.27 cm) ginger, piece, peeled

3 cups (675g) garden greens, packed - kale, spinach, lettuce, etc.

2 tablespoons (30 ml) maple syrup, optional

DIRECTIONS

Place all of the ingredients in the blender in the order they are listed.

Note: I put half of the greens in until they get blended down somewhat and then add the rest.

Blend for at least one minute or until everything is well blended and smooth.

Serve immediately.

SERVINGS: 3
CALORIES PER SERVING: 193
PROTEIN PER SERVING: 2.78 GRAMS

VERY BERRY SMOOTHIE

Can you have too many berries? We sure don't think so. These super foods are tasty, sweet and really, really good for you.

Try it without the maple syrup first. We sure find it sweet enough that way.

INGREDIENTS

1½ cups (350 ml) almond milk (or plant-based milk of your choice)

½ cup (50g) blueberries, fresh or frozen

½ cup (100g) strawberries, fresh or frozen

½ cup (65g) raspberries, fresh or frozen

½ cup (65g) blackberries, fresh or frozen

1 medium banana, fresh or frozen

1 tablespoon (15 ml) ground flax seed

2 tablespoons (30 ml) maple syrup, optional

1 cup (about 8 cubes) ice cubes

DIRECTIONS

Place all the ingredients in your blender in the order given.

Make sure the lid is secure and start at the lowest speed, gradually increasing to maximum speed.

Blend for at least one minute or until all ingredients are smooth and well blended.

Serve immediately.

SERVINGS: 4
CALORIES PER SERVING: 116
PROTEIN PER SERVING: 1.73 GRAMS

EASY GREEN SMOOTHIE

*T*his smoothie makes it easy to get your greens and your protein. As a bonus, it tastes great, too!

INGREDIENTS

1 cup (240 ml) oat milk (or plant-based milk of your choice)

3 prunes

1 wedge cantaloupe (about ⅛ medium cantaloupe)

1 cup (225g) baby spinach

1 banana, fresh or frozen

1 kiwi, peeled

⅓ cup (25g) old fashioned rolled oats

⅓ cup (35g) blueberries, fresh or frozen

DIRECTIONS

Place all the ingredients in your blender in the order given.

Make sure the lid is secure and start at the lowest speed, gradually increasing to maximum speed.

Blend for at least one minute or until all ingredients are smooth and well blended.

Serve immediately.

SERVINGS: 2
CALORIES PER SERVING: 281
PROTEIN PER SERVING: 7.51 GRAMS

LUNCH RECIPES

*E*asy, tasty, vegan lunches can be easier than you think.

Chickpea "No-Egg" Salad

$\mathcal{O}$nce you've tried this you won't even miss the standard egg salad. Make a sandwich or a wrap and serve with a side salad or coleslaw.

INGREDIENTS

1½ cups (300g) chickpeas, cooked, drained, homemade or canned

2 cloves garlic, minced

2 tablespoons (30 ml) red onion, minced

2 tablespoons (30 ml) celery, minced

¼ teaspoon (1.25 ml) turmeric

¼ teaspoon (1.25 ml) paprika

¼ teaspoon (1.25 ml) salt

3 tablespoons (45 ml) mayonnaise, vegan

black pepper, to taste

DIRECTIONS

Pulse the chickpeas 3 or 4 times in a food processor until they are a combination of small chunks and smooth.

Add the rest of the ingredients and mix until smooth.

Make a sandwich or wrap. Alternately, serve on a bed of mixed greens.

SERVINGS: 4

CALORIES PER SERVING (SALAD ONLY): 159

PROTEIN PER SERVING (SALAD ONLY): 4.59 GRAMS

BLACK BEANS AND TOMATOES

Sometimes the simplest recipes are the tastiest. We like to keep pre-cooked black beans in the freezer so we have something to use for a quick meal. We frequently pre-cook a pound or two of black beans ahead of time and then package them up in 1½ to 2 cup (90g to 120g) portions and freeze them. Perfect for almost any recipe.

This recipe is packed with protein and is great on its own or served with toast, pasta, rice or potato.

As a bonus, it can be made ahead, refrigerated and served cold over your choice of mixed greens.

INGREDIENTS

2 tablespoons (30 ml) water or vegetable broth

2 cloves garlic, finely diced

1 small onion, chopped

1 stalk celery, sliced

½ medium bell pepper, chopped

1 large tomato, diced

3 ounces (85g) tomato paste

3 dashes tabasco sauce

1 teaspoon (5 ml) balsamic vinegar

1½ cups (90g) black beans, cooked

Chopped cilantro, chives or green onions for garnish, if desired.

DIRECTIONS

Heat a skillet over medium-high heat.

Add the water (or broth) and then add the garlic, onions, celery and bell pepper.

Cook until everything softens slightly, about 3-4 minutes.

Add the diced tomato and cook for another minute or two.

Add the tomato paste, tabasco sauce and balsamic vinegar. Stir until everything is well combined.

Add the black beans and stir well.

Continue to cook until the beans are warmed through and the sauce is bubbling.

Remove from heat and serve immediately. Garnish as desired.

Or, refrigerate or freeze for later use.

SERVINGS: 2
CALORIES PER SERVING: 257
PROTEIN PER SERVING: 15.78 GRAMS

Basic Baked Beans in a Slow Cooker

Another significant source of protein, baked beans, are a staple at our house. They make a great lunch on their own with some toast or warmed pitas. They can also be used as a side dish to enhance many other meals, too.

INGREDIENTS

1½ pounds (680g) dried navy beans, or Great Northern beans

water, for soaking and boiling

2 cups (475 ml) water

1 large yellow onion, chopped

1 large carrot, diced

½ medium green bell pepper, diced

1 rib celery, diced

¾ cup (180 ml) tomato paste

¾ cup (180 ml) maple syrup, NOT pancake syrup!

3 tablespoons (45 ml) brown sugar, packed

2 teaspoons (10 ml) dry mustard, optional

1 teaspoon (5 ml) sea salt

1 teaspoon (5 ml) black pepper, freshly ground

1 inch (2.54 cm) ginger, grated

DIRECTIONS

In a large saucepan, soak the dried beans overnight in enough water to cover the beans by about an inch.

In the morning, drain the beans and discard the soak water. Return the beans to the large saucepan and again cover with water. Bring to a boil, reduce the heat and simmer for 30 minutes.

Drain the beans and put them in your slow cooker. Add all of the remaining ingredients and stir well.

Note: for the 2 cups (475 ml) of water called for in the recipe, we like to use water saved from cooking or steaming vegetables, or vegetable broth.

Turn your slow cooker to high for the first hour, then reduce the heat to low and allow the beans to cook for 6-7 hours.

Check the beans from time to time, giving them a stir and adding additional liquid, if required.

The beans are ready when they are tender and most of the liquid has been absorbed.

SERVINGS: 10
CALORIES PER SERVING: 338
PROTEIN PER SERVING: 16.58 GRAMS

BABY SPINACH SALAD

Spinach grows well in our garden. We make a lot a spinach salads when it's in season.

INGREDIENTS

2 cups (450g) baby spinach leaves, packed

1 large pear

1 teaspoon (5 ml) lemon juice, freshly squeezed

½ cup (100g) chickpeas

¼ cup (30g) walnut pieces

2 tablespoons (30 ml) raisins

4 tablespoons (60 ml) extra virgin olive oil

3 tablespoons (45 ml) apple cider vinegar

2 tablespoons (30 ml) maple syrup

1 sprig fresh rosemary

sea salt, to taste

black pepper, freshly ground, to taste

DIRECTIONS

Wash the spinach well and spin or pat dry.

Wash the pear, cut it in quarters, core it and coarsely chop it. Toss the chopped pear in the lemon juice to prevent it from going brown.

In a large salad bowl, combine the spinach, pear, chickpeas, walnuts and raisins. Toss to mix.

In a separate bowl, whisk together the olive oil, vinegar and maple syrup. Remove the leaves from the sprig of Rosemary and add them to the oil and vinegar mixture. Whisk again. Add the salt and pepper to taste and whisk once more.

Gently pour the oil and vinegar mixture over the salad and toss lightly to combine.

Serve immediately.

SERVINGS: 2
CALORIES PER SERVING: 442
PROTEIN PER SERVING: 7.31 GRAMS

MEXICAN STYLE BEAN SALAD

This is a zesty twist on a traditional bean salad.

INGREDIENTS

1 cup (170g) kidney beans, cooked

1 cup (164g) chickpeas, cooked

1 cup (75g) baby lima beans, cooked

1 cup (172g) black beans, cooked

1 cup (175g) corn, fresh, frozen or canned

1½ cups (180g) green beans, cooked, straight cut

½ medium red onion, diced

2 stalks celery, diced

¼ medium green bell pepper, diced

¼ medium red bell pepper, diced

2 garlic cloves, minced

1 jalapeño, diced

5 leaves cilantro, chopped

½ cup (120 ml) extra virgin olive oil

½ cup (120 ml) white vinegar

¼ cup (60 ml) balsamic vinegar

½ cup (100g) granulated sugar

1 tablespoon (15 ml) lime juice, freshly squeezed

1½ teaspoons (7.5 ml) sea salt

1 teaspoon (5 ml) black pepper, freshly ground

DIRECTIONS

All the beans in this recipe were cooked from dried beans with the exception, of course, for the green beans and corn. They were cooked from fresh.

You can substitute canned beans and corn in the recipe if it's easier for you. Just be sure to rinse the canned beans very well to eliminate any unwanted salt.

In a large glass bowl, combine all the beans, corn, red onion, celery, and peppers.

Note: you don't want to use metal bowls when using vinegar. You could use plastic but glass works much better.

In a large measuring cup, combine the olive oil, vinegars, sugar, lime juice, salt and pepper. Whisk well until ingredients are well combined and most of the sugar has dissolved.

Pour the oil and vinegar mixture over the bean mixture and stir well with a wooden spoon.

Cover the bean salad and refrigerate for at least 4 hours before serving. This allows all the flavors to blend and mature.

SERVINGS: 10
CALORIES PER SERVING: 253
PROTEIN PER SERVING: 6.23 GRAMS

VEGAN CARROT HOT DOGS

$\mathcal{B}$e sure to get these puppies marinating at least 24 hours before you plan to eat them to get the most robust flavor.

You can grill them or heat them in a skillet and just add a whole grain bun and your favorite condiments.

We like to have them with some homemade coleslaw on the side.

INGREDIENTS

4 large carrots, peeled and tops and bottoms removed (try to use ones that are a consistent size and thickness)

MARINADE INGREDIENTS

½ cup (120 ml) soy sauce

½ cup (120 ml) apple cider vinegar, preferably with "the Mother"

½ cup (120 ml) vegetable broth or water

2 tablespoons (30 ml) pure maple syrup (the real stuff - NOT pancake syrup)

2 teaspoons (10 ml) smoked paprika

2 teaspoons (10 ml) garlic powder

2 teaspoons (10 ml) onion powder

½ teaspoon (2.5 ml) liquid smoke

½ teaspoon (2.5 ml) black pepper, freshly ground

DIRECTIONS

Steam (or boil) the carrots until they are fork-tender. Depending on the size and thickness of the carrots, this can take 30-40 minutes.

Drain the carrots and set aside.

In a medium bowl, add all the marinade ingredients and whisk together until well combined.

Combine the carrots and marinade in an appropriate size, covered, dish or container. You want to be sure that the carrots are completely covered by the marinade.

Refrigerate for 24 hours.

When ready to cook, drain the carrots, reserving the marinade.

Either cook them on a hot grill, or in a skillet over medium-high heat, until golden brown - about 5 to 10 minutes. Remember, they just need to be heated through.

You can use the reserved marinade to make more carrot hot dogs or save it add it to other recipes.

Place carrots in buns and serve with condiments of your choice, such as:

- ketchup
- mustard
- sauerkraut
- chopped onions
- green relish
- etc.

STATS FOR CARROT DOGS ONLY

SERVINGS: 4

CALORIES PER SERVING: 92 - ACTUALLY, THIS IS NOT TOTALLY ACCURATE AS THIS INCLUDES THE INGREDIENTS IN THE MARINADE AND YOU DON'T USE ALL OF IT.

PROTEIN PER SERVING: 3.84 GRAMS

DINNER RECIPES

Here are lots of dinner recipes that are easy to make and will even "wow" some of your non-vegan friends and family.

Roasted Cauliflower Dinner

auliflower is probably one of our favorite veggies and this complete Roasted Cauliflower Dinner is, quite simply, amazing.

The combination of flavors and textures will make you want to make this meal again and again.

Carve the cauliflower into slices and serve with the roasted veggies and gravy.

For the Gravy

2 cups (475 ml) vegetable broth

¼ cup (60 ml) soy sauce

1 tablespoon (15 ml) maple syrup

2 teaspoons (10 ml) vegan Worcestershire sauce

4 cloves garlic, minced

¼ medium yellow onion, minced

1 tablespoon (15 ml) parsley, fresh, minced or 1 tsp (5 ml) dried

½ teaspoon (2.5 ml) thyme

½ teaspoon (2.5 ml) sage

½ teaspoon (2.5 ml) smoked paprika

½ teaspoon (2.5 ml) black pepper, freshly ground

3 tablespoons (45 ml) cornstarch

¼ cup (60 ml) water

For the Roast

1 large cauliflower, whole, leaves trimmed

4 large carrots, peeled and chunked

4 large parsnips, peeled and chunked

6 medium red potatoes, scrubbed and chunked

½ cup (120 ml) vegetable broth

DIRECTIONS

Making the Gravy

In a medium-sized pot, whisk together all of the gravy ingredients EXCEPT for the cornstarch and water.

Bring to a boil and then turn down to a simmer on medium-low heat for 5 minutes. (This will allow all the flavors to marry.) Remove from the heat.

In a separate bowl, whisk together the cornstarch and water to make a cornstarch slurry.

Once the pot is no longer simmering, slowly whisk the cornstarch slurry into the gravy a little at a time. Going slow will ensure that no clumps form.

The gravy will begin to thicken as soon as the cornstarch is whisked in. Put the pot back on the stove and return to a simmer for an additional 3 minutes.

Making the Roast

Pre-heat the oven to 450°F (230°C, Gas Mark 8).

Arrange the potatoes, parsnips and carrots in a roasting dish with the cauliflower in the center. Be careful not to overcrowd the dish.

Place the cauliflower upside-down and pour ⅓ cup (80 ml) of the gravy into it. Give it a good shake to distribute the gravy.

Place the cauliflower right-side up and brush more gravy on the top to cover it - about ⅓ to ½ cup (80 to 120 ml).

Add ½ cup (120 ml) of vegetable stock to the bottom of the dish (this will help steam the veggies.)

Pour about a ⅓ cup (80 ml) of gravy over top of the potatoes, parsnips and carrots.

Cover the dish tightly with a lid or aluminum foil and bake for 40 minutes, brushing the cauliflower with more gravy halfway through.

Uncover the cauliflower roast and brush more gravy on. Bake for another 30 minutes (uncovered), brushing with more gravy halfway again.

Remove from the oven and serve while hot.

SERVINGS: 6
CALORIES PER SERVING: 316
PROTEIN PER SERVING: 9.31 GRAMS

Geoff's Favorite No-Meat Loaf

*T*his is one of our "go to" recipes. Leftovers freeze well and can be microwaved in a pinch, so we always like to have some in the freezer. Serve it with your favorite veggies and a nice vegan gravy, too.

INGREDIENTS

2 cups (475 ml) vegetable broth, preferably homemade

¾ cup (150g) green lentils

¼ cup (55g) bulgur wheat

2 tablespoons (30 ml) ground flax seed

½ cup (120 ml) water

½ cup (120 ml) crushed tomato

2 tablespoons (30 ml) tomato paste

½ cup (100g) chickpeas, lightly mashed

1 tablespoon (15 ml) Italian seasoning

½ small red onion, chopped

4 shakes hot pepper sauce

¼ medium red bell pepper, chopped

1 cup (90g) oatmeal, quick

1 teaspoon (5 ml) black pepper, freshly ground

1 teaspoon (5 ml) sea salt

DIRECTIONS

In a medium saucepan, bring the broth to a boil. Add the lentils and bulgur wheat, reduce heat and cover. Cook for 30 minutes, until soft. Remove from heat and allow to cool completely.

Once the lentils and bulgur wheat have cooled, mix the ground flax seed and water together and allow to sit for about 5 minutes until it thickens.

Pre-heat the oven to 375°F (190°C, Gas Mark 5) and lightly oil a glass loaf pan or line the loaf pan with parchment paper (our preferred method).

In a large bowl, mix together the cooled lentils and bulgar wheat. Add all of the other ingredients, including the flax/water mixture. Mix well.

Place the mixture in the prepared loaf pan and pat down, smoothing out the top.

Bake at 375°F (190°C, Gas Mark 5) for 45 minutes, until the top is well browned.

Allow the loaf to cool for 10 minutes before slicing.

SERVINGS: 8

CALORIES PER SERVING: 158

PROTEIN PER SERVING: 8.14 GRAMS

Tip: You can make the gravy from the Roasted Cauliflower Dinner recipe for this recipe as well.

CHICKPEA POT PIE

his recipe makes two complete pies. Any leftovers freeze well.

These taste so much like a regular chicken pot pie that you won't even miss the chicken.

We like to serve this pie with mashed potatoes, steamed veggies and some homemade cranberry sauce on the side.

INGREDIENTS

2 cups (300g) red onion, diced

2 cups (400g) chickpeas, cooked and drained (a 28-oz can)

2 cups (300g) frozen peas

2 cups (350g) frozen corn

1 tablespoon (15 ml) poultry seasoning

1 tablespoon (15 ml) Herbes de Provence (or mixed herbs of your choice)

2 - 10.5 ounce cans (310 ml) vegan mushroom soup

1 cup (240 ml) non-dairy milk

1 teaspoon (5 ml) black pepper, freshly ground

1 teaspoon (5 ml) sea salt

Enough vegan pastry for 4 pie crusts

DIRECTIONS

Preheat the oven to 425°F (220°C, Gas Mark 7).

In a large bowl, mash the chickpeas a little bit so you still have about half of the chickpeas intact.

Add the rest of the ingredients, except the pastry, and mix well.

Line 2 - 8-9-inch (20-23 cm) deep pie plates with half of the prepared pastry.

Fill each of the pies with half of the filling mixture.

Top each pie with the remaining pastry, seal the edges and vent the tops.

Bake at 425°F (220°C, Gas Mark 7) for 45-50 minutes or until golden brown and bubbly.

Remove from the oven to a heatproof surface and allow to cool for about 10 minutes before cutting into serving sizes.

Serve with sides of your choice.

SERVINGS: 12 (6 PER PIE)
CALORIES PER SERVING: 454
PROTEIN PER SERVING: 6.82 GRAMS

ROASTED ROOT VEGETABLES

We like to make this dish in the autumn with root vegetables pulled from our own garden. Veggies that are that fresh just explode with flavor. But this is good anytime of year, too. So, don't limit yourself to the Fall.

INGREDIENTS

2 tablespoons (30 ml) coconut oil

1 large yellow onion, quartered

4 medium potatoes, chunked

3 large carrots, peeled and chopped

3 large parsnips, peeled and chunked

½ medium rutabaga, peeled and chunked

1 tablespoon (15 ml) Herbes de Provence or herb mix of your choice or fresh herbs of your choice

DIRECTIONS

Place the coconut oil in an 11" x 13" (28 cm x 33 cm) glass baking dish.

Place the dish in a cold oven and then preheat the oven to 425°F (220°C, Gas Mark 7), with the glass dish in the oven.

Once the oven has reached 425°F (220°C, Gas Mark 7), carefully remove it from the oven to a heatproof surface.

Toss all of the vegetables in the hot oil, ensuring they are all evenly coated with the oil.

Add the herbs and toss again.

Return the dish to the oven.

Toss the vegetables every 20 minutes until they are well browned - approximately one hour.

When done, remove the dish from the oven and serve the vegetables immediately.

Salt and pepper the veggies to taste.

SERVINGS: 6
CALORIES PER SERVING: 318
PROTEIN PER SERVING: 6.81 GRAMS

VEGAN ROASTED VEGETABLE MEDLEY

Not quite Ratatouille and not quite Vegetable Tian, but something in between and just as tasty as either one.

This dish is colorful, tasty, easy to make and pretty impressive, too.

INGREDIENTS

½ cup (120 ml) tomato sauce (we used our homemade Tomato Basil Sauce)

1 medium eggplant

1 large zucchini

2 medium tomatoes

1 medium red pepper

1 medium green pepper

1 medium yam (sweet potato)

2 small red potatoes

1 medium red onion

2 tablespoons (30 ml) olive oil

1 tablespoon (15 ml) garlic, minced

1 tablespoon (15 ml) Italian seasoning

¼ cup (15g) nutritional yeast

chives, for garnish

DIRECTIONS

Prepare all of the vegetables by slicing them all about ¼" (0.6 cm) thick.

Note: Some of the vegetables will need to be halved, lengthwise, because of their size, before slicing.

Coat an 11" x 13" (28 cm x 33 cm) glass baking dish with non-stick cooking spray and spread the tomato sauce in the bottom.

Standing the sliced veggies on their edge, place one slice of each type of veggie together and then continue the pattern until the entire dish is filled.

Combine the olive oil, garlic and Italian seasoning and mix well. Baste the top of the veggies with this mixture.

Cover the dish with foil and bake, at 350°F (180°C, Gas Mark 4), for 30 minutes.

After 30 minutes, remove the foil and return the dish to the oven and bake for an additional 30 minutes.

After the additional 30 minutes, remove from the oven, garnish with the nutritional yeast and chopped chives and serve immediately.

SERVINGS: 6
CALORIES PER SERVING: 207
PROTEIN PER SERVING: 7.44 GRAMS

BLACK BEAN STEW IN A SLOW COOKER

*F*or this recipe we used frozen tomatoes and zucchini from our garden. We have always said, the best way to get organic produce is to grow it yourself. If you're using vegetables you've frozen yourself, be sure to let them thaw in a colander and catch any of the water that runs off. Save the water to add to your homemade vegetable broth. Thawing the veggies this way will make them a little firmer and they'll stand up in the stew a little better.

Naturally, this recipe works just fine with fresh vegetables, too.

INGREDIENTS

6 tomatoes, chopped

1 small zucchini, chopped

1 medium yellow onion, chopped

1 jalapeño pepper, chopped

2 stalks celery, sliced

¼ cup (60 ml) tomato paste

¼ cup (60 ml) sun dried tomatoes, chopped

3 tablespoons (45 ml) taco seasoning

½ cup (90g) corn

2 cups (120g) black beans, home cooked or canned, drained and rinsed

1 cup (67g) kale, packed, chopped (you can substitute spinach or beet greens, if you prefer)

1 teaspoon (5 ml) pepper

DIRECTIONS

Combined all ingredients in the slow cooker except the kale. Stir well.

Set slow cooker on high for one hour and then reduce to low. Cook on low for an additional 4-5 hours.

Add the kale and stir well. Turn the slow cooker back to high for about 30 minutes, then reduce to low for another 30 minutes.

Serve over brown rice, pasta or potatoes.

SERVINGS: 4
CALORIES PER SERVING: 229
PROTEIN PER SERVING: 12.97 GRAMS

Beet Green and Red Cabbage Slow Cooker Meal

A meal you can set-and-forget is always a plus for those particularly busy days. And this amazing dinner ticks all the boxes for not only protein but all kinds of nutrients your body needs.

Have as is, or serve with a hearty bread, some whole grain pasta or some brown rice.

INGREDIENTS

1 small yellow onion, sliced

2 cloves garlic, minced

2 stalks celery, sliced

2 large carrots, cut into chunks

½ medium green pepper, chopped

¼ head red cabbage, thinly sliced

1 inch (2.54 cm) ginger, piece, minced

1 bunch beet greens, sliced

2 cups (400g) chickpeas, cooked

1½ cups (350 ml) vegetable broth

2 tablespoons (30 ml) balsamic vinegar

2 tablespoons (30 ml) brown sugar

1 medium apple, cored and chopped

1 teaspoon (5 ml) sea salt

1 teaspoon (5 ml) black pepper, freshly ground

DIRECTIONS

Combined all ingredients in the slow cooker. Stir well.

Set slow cooker on high for one hour and then reduce to low. Cook on low for an additional 4-5 hours.

Serve over brown rice, pasta or potatoes.

SERVINGS: 4
CALORIES PER SERVING: 235
PROTEIN PER SERVING: 8.62 GRAMS

LATIN-INSPIRED BEAN STEW

The jalapeño in this recipe helps to give this dish a little "kick". Use more, or less, depending on the amount of heat you prefer.

INGREDIENTS

1 cup (240 ml) tomato juice or vegetable cocktail

2 cups (475 ml) water

1½ cups (340g) brown rice

2 tablespoons (30 ml) olive oil

1 large onion, chopped

2 stalks celery, sliced

4 cloves garlic, minced

2 medium sweet potatoes (yams), peeled and chunked

1½ cups (350 ml) water

2 cups (120g) cooked black beans

2 cups (120g) cooked black-eyed beans

½ large red bell pepper, diced

½ large green bell pepper, diced

1 cup (200g) tomatoes, diced

1 cup (125g) yellow squash, chopped

1 cup (175g) corn, fresh or frozen

1 jalapeño, diced

¼ cup (5g) fresh parsley, chopped

1 teaspoon (5 ml) sea salt

DIRECTIONS

In a large saucepan, combine the tomato juice, 2 cups (475 ml) of water and rice.

Cover and bring to a boil, then reduce the heat and simmer gently until all the liquid has been absorbed - about 35-40 minutes.

In a large soup pot, heat the oil over medium-high heat.

Add the onion and celery. Sauté until the onion is translucent - about 5 minutes.

Add the garlic and continue to sauté until the onion begins to brown.

Add the chunked sweet potatoes to the pot and stir well.

Add 1½ cups (350 ml) warm water.

Bring the ingredients to a simmer and simmer, covered, until the sweet potatoes are tender but still firm - about 10 - 15 minutes.

Add the rest of the ingredients, except the parsley and salt.

Return to a simmer, cover and simmer gently for an additional 15 minutes.

Remove the lid for the last 5 minutes.

Add the parsley and salt, stir well.

Serve immediately with the tomato rice.

SERVINGS: 6
CALORIES PER SERVING: 483
PROTEIN PER SERVING: 16.46 GRAMS

Italian Bean Casserole

You can use any kind of pasta you choose for this recipe. We used elbow macaroni. If you use spaghetti or some other long noodle, be sure to break it up into smaller pieces.

This nutritious casserole is high in protein and fiber, thanks to the beans, and has no added fat.

INGREDIENTS

1 cup (200g) great Northern Beans, dry

1 cup (200g) small red beans, dry

5 cups (1.2 L) cold water

28 ounces (796 ml) diced tomatoes, canned

1 medium yellow onion, chopped

1 stalk celery, chopped

4 cups (950 ml) vegetable broth

3 cloves garlic, minced

1 tablespoon (15 ml) Italian seasoning

½ teaspoon (2.5 ml) black pepper, freshly ground

1½ teaspoons (7.5 ml) sea salt

1 medium zucchini, chopped

8 ounces (226g) pasta, your choice

DIRECTIONS

In a large pot, combine the dry beans with approximately 5 cups (1.2L) of cold water. Bring the beans to a boil, reduce the heat and simmer for 2 minutes. Remove from the heat and let sit, covered, for 1 hour. Then drain and rinse the beans.

Add all the ingredients, with the exception of the zucchini and pasta, to your slow cooker. Stir well to combine. Set the slow cooker on high for the first hour and then reduce to low.

Cook on low for approximately 8-9 hours, then increase to high and add the zucchini and pasta. Cook for an additional hour on high. The pasta should be tender and the zucchini should be cooked.

Serve hot.

This casserole freezes well.

SERVINGS: 6
CALORIES PER SERVING: 414
PROTEIN PER SERVING: 21.38 GRAMS

VEGETABLE STIR FRY

With all these veggies, this recipe makes for a satisfying and filling meal. You can pair it with some organic brown rice, if desired.

INGREDIENTS

1 teaspoon (5 ml) olive oil

1 medium yellow onion, halved and sliced

4 cloves garlic, minced

½ inch (1.3 cm) fresh ginger, piece, minced

2 medium carrots, cut into matchsticks

2 stalks celery, sliced

¼ medium cabbage, sliced

1 cup (175g) broccoli, chopped

½ large green bell pepper, chopped

½ large red bell pepper, chopped

1 cup (150g) sugar snap peas

1 medium zucchini, halved and sliced

6 mushrooms, sliced

STIR FRY SAUCE INGREDIENTS

¼ cup (60 ml) soy sauce

1 tablespoon (15 ml) balsamic vinegar

¼ cup (60 ml) maple syrup

½ cup (120 ml) vegetable broth

¼ teaspoon (1.25 ml) cayenne pepper

DIRECTIONS

Combine all the ingredients for the stir fry sauce in a container with a lid. Shake well and set aside.

Over medium-high heat, heat the oil in a large wok or deep frying pan. Add the garlic and ginger and cook for a minute or two.

Add the onion, carrots and celery and stir fry for 4 to 5 minutes, then add the cabbage and the broccoli and stir fry for another 3 to 4 minutes.

Add all of the stir fry sauce and mix well. Cover and cook for 5 minutes.

Add the zucchini, peppers, mushrooms and sugar snap peas, stir and cover. Continue to cook for another 4-5 minutes.

Remove from heat and serve over rice.

SERVINGS: 4

CALORIES PER SERVING (NOT INCLUDING RICE): 181

PROTEIN PER SERVING (NOT INCLUDING RICE): 8.24 GRAMS

GERMAN-STYLE RED LENTIL DINNER

INGREDIENTS

4 cups (950 ml) vegetable broth, preferably homemade, divided

1 small yellow onion, chopped

2 medium leeks, white parts only, halved and sliced

2 stalks celery, sliced

4 cloves garlic, minced

1 teaspoon (5 ml) thyme

1 teaspoon (5 ml) caraway seed

3 cups (600g) red lentils, rinsed

2 medium red potatoes, chopped

2 medium carrots, peeled and chopped

1 teaspoon (5 ml) sea salt, or to taste

1 teaspoon (5 ml) black pepper, freshly ground, to taste

DIRECTIONS

In a large saucepan, heat about ¼ cup (60 ml) of the vegetable broth over medium heat.

Add the onion, leeks, celery garlic, thyme and caraway and sauté for 3-4 minutes

Add the lentils and sauté for another 1-2 minutes.

Add the potatoes and carrots and sauté for another 1-2 minutes.

Add the rest of the vegetable broth and bring to a boil.

Reduce heat, cover and simmer for approximately 35 minutes.

Season with salt and freshly ground black pepper.

Serve immediately.

This recipe freezes well.

SERVINGS: 8
CALORIES PER SERVING: 327
PROTEIN PER SERVING: 19.6 GRAMS

Simple Roasted Butternut Squash

1 butternut squash - peeled, seeded, and cut into 1-inch cubes

2 tablespoons (30 ml) olive oil

2 cloves garlic, minced

salt and ground black pepper to taste

DIRECTIONS

Preheat oven to 400°F (200°C, Gas Mark 6).

Toss butternut squash with olive oil and garlic in a large bowl. Season with salt and black pepper. Arrange coated squash on a baking sheet.

Roast in the preheated oven until squash is tender and lightly browned, 25 to 30 minutes.

SERVINGS: 4
CALORIES PER SERVING: 124
PROTEIN PER SERVING: 1.50 GRAMS

SEITAN RECIPES - AKA "FAKE" MEAT

Seitan is a great substitute for meat. It's vegan and you're not going to believe the amount of protein you'll get per serving.

Sadly, if you're gluten-intolerant, you'll need to skip any of these seitan recipes as their main ingredient is Vital Wheat Gluten. But, for those of us who are fine with gluten, you're going to want to try these.

SEITAN ROAST BEEPH

No, Beeph is not a typo. This recipe makes a roast that tastes like beef and slices like beef. And it's vegan!

Not only that - check out how much protein this "fake" meat has!

You can use it for dinner - roast beeph, mashed potatoes, veggies and, yes, even gravy!

Don't let the long list of ingredients and directions intimidate you, it's actually pretty easy to make.

INGREDIENTS

2 cups (242g) vital wheat gluten

½ cup (45g) chickpea flour

½ cup (30g) nutritional yeast

1 tablespoon (15 ml) smoked paprika

1 tablespoon (15 ml) basil

1 tablespoon (15 ml) onion powder

1 tablespoon (15 ml) tomato paste

2 tablespoons (30 ml) Worcestershire sauce, vegan

½ cup (120 ml) soy sauce

1½ cups (350 ml) hot water

4 cups (950 ml) vegetable broth, preferably home made

1 tablespoon (15 ml) vegan beef flavoring

DIRECTIONS

In a large bowl, whisk together the vital wheat gluten, chickpea flour (aka garbanzo bean flour or besan), nutritional yeast , smoked paprika, basil and onion powder.

Set aside.

In a large measuring cup (we use a 4-cup (950 ml) measuring cup), whisk together the tomato paste, Worcestershire sauce, soy sauce and hot water.

Add the wet ingredients to the dry ingredients and stir until it starts to hold together. (This can happen pretty quickly.)

Knead the seitan for 4 to 5 minutes. Add more vital wheat gluten if the dough is too sticky.

Shape the seitan into a "roast" shape that will easily fit in the large saucepan or Dutch oven you'll be using to simmer the roast.

In a large saucepan or Dutch oven, combine the vegetable broth and vegan beef flavoring. Stir well.

Bring the broth to a boil.

While waiting for the broth to come to a boil, wrap the roast in enough cheesecloth to cover it with 2-3 layers.

Seal the ends with string.

When the broth is boiling, gently lower the roast into the pot, let the broth come back to a boil, then cover the pot and reduce the heat to a simmer.

Simmer the roast for approximately one hour, turning it every 15 minutes.

After an hour, turn off the heat and allow the roast to cool, in the broth for an additional 15 minutes.

Carefully remove the roast to a heatproof surface and allow it to cool completely.

Or, you can actually slice it while it's still warm and serve immediately.

We actually like to let it cool and then refrigerate it, to make slicing easier, then re-heat it later. We also find that the flavor matures if you let it sit in the fridge for several hours, or overnight.

REMEMBER - DON'T THROW AWAY THE BROTH.

Simply thickening the broth with a little cornstarch makes a nice gravy. You can also add additional spices, if you desire.

TIP:

While this recipe is certainly easy to make by hand, we prefer to mix it in a stand mixer and do the kneading part with a dough hook. It comes out great!

> SERVINGS: 14
> CALORIES PER SERVING: 168
> PROTEIN PER SERVING: 28.83 GRAMS

Seitan Roast Beeph with Jackfruit

This recipe is pretty much the same as the one above but with the addition of some jackfruit to give it more of a "stringy" texture like the grain in a beef roast. It's still just as easy to make, too!

INGREDIENTS

2 cups (242g) vital wheat gluten

½ cup (45g) chickpea flour

½ cup (30g) nutritional yeast

1 tablespoon (15 ml) smoked paprika

1 tablespoon (15 ml) basil

1 tablespoon (15 ml) onion powder

1½ cups (226g) jackfruit, approx. a 10-ounce can, packed in brine, rinsed

1 tablespoon (15 ml) tomato paste

2 tablespoons (30 ml) Worcestershire sauce, vegan

½ cup (120 ml) soy sauce

1½ cups (350 ml) hot water

4 cups (950 ml) vegetable broth, preferably home made

1 tablespoon (15 ml) vegan beef flavoring

DIRECTIONS

In a large bowl, whisk together the vital wheat gluten, chickpea flour (aka besan), nutritional yeast , smoked paprika, basil and onion powder.

Set aside.

Drain and rinse the jackfruit. Place it in a food processor and pulse the chunks 3 or 4 times. It doesn't take much for them to separate into "fibers".

In a large measuring cup (we use a 4-cup measuring cup), whisk together the tomato paste, Worcestershire sauce, soy sauce and hot water. Then add the prepared jackfruit and stir well.

Add the wet ingredients to the dry ingredients and stir until it starts to hold together. (This can happen pretty quickly.)

Knead the seitan for 4 to 5 minutes. Add more vital wheat gluten if the dough is too sticky. (We found, with the addition of the jackfruit, that we needed to add ¼ to ½ cup (15g to 30g) of extra Vital Wheat Gluten.)

Shape the seitan into a "roast" shape that will easily fit in the large saucepan or Dutch oven you'll be using to simmer the roast in.

In a large saucepan or Dutch oven, combine the vegetable broth and vegan beef flavoring. Stir well.

Bring the broth to a boil.

While waiting for the broth to come to a boil, wrap the roast in enough cheesecloth to cover it with 2-3 layers.

Seal the ends with string.

When the broth is boiling, gently lower the roast into the pot, let the broth come back to a boil, then cover the pot and reduce the heat to a simmer.

Simmer the roast for approximately one hour, turning it every 15 minutes.

After an hour, turn off the heat and allow the roast to cool, in the broth for an additional 15 minutes.

Carefully remove the roast to a heatproof surface and allow it to cool completely.

Or, you can actually slice it while it's still warm and serve immediately.

We actually like to let it cool and then refrigerate it, to make slicing easier, then re-heat it later. We also find that the flavor matures if you let it sit in the fridge for several hours, or overnight.

REMEMBER - DON'T THROW AWAY THE BROTH.

Simply thickening the broth with a little cornstarch makes a nice gravy. You can also add additional spices, if you desire.

TIP:

While this recipe is certainly easy to make by hand, we prefer to mix it in a stand mixer and do the kneading part with a dough hook. It comes out great!

SERVINGS: 14
CALORIES PER SERVING: 224
PROTEIN PER SERVING: 29.85 GRAMS

Seitan Roast Chik'n

The spices in this rendition give it the essence of roast chicken. It's great sliced up for sandwiches, or for dinner with some gravy made from the cooking broth. It can also be used in a stir fry or pretty much anywhere else you used to use cooked chicken.

INGREDIENTS

2 cups (242g) vital wheat gluten

½ cup (45g) chickpea flour

½ cup (30g) nutritional yeast

1 tablespoon (15 ml) smoked paprika

1 tablespoon (15 ml) poultry seasoning

1 tablespoon (15 ml) onion powder

1 tablespoon (15 ml) tomato paste

1 teaspoon (5 ml) sea salt

2 tablespoons (30 ml) Worcestershire sauce, vegan

½ cup (120 ml) soy sauce

1½ cups (350 ml) hot water

4 cups (950 ml) vegetable broth, preferably home made

1 tablespoon (15 ml) poultry seasoning

DIRECTIONS

In a large bowl, whisk together the vital wheat gluten, chickpea flour (aka garbanzo bean flour or besan), nutritional yeast , smoked paprika, poultry seasoning, onion powder and salt.

Set aside.

In a large measuring cup (we use a 4-cup (950 ml) measuring cup), whisk together the tomato paste, Worcestershire sauce, soy sauce and hot water.

Add the wet ingredients to the dry ingredients and stir until it starts to hold together. (This can happen pretty quickly.)

Knead the seitan for 4 to 5 minutes. Add more vital wheat gluten if the dough is too sticky.

Shape the seitan into a "roast" shape that will easily fit in the large saucepan or Dutch oven you'll be using to simmer the roast.

In a large saucepan or Dutch oven, combine the vegetable broth and poultry seasoning. Stir well.

Bring the broth to a boil.

While waiting for the broth to come to a boil, wrap the roast in enough cheesecloth to cover it with 2-3 layers.

Seal the ends with string.

When the broth is boiling, gently lower the roast into the pot, let the broth come back to a boil, then cover the pot and reduce the heat to a simmer.

Simmer the roast for approximately one hour, turning it every 15 minutes.

After an hour, turn off the heat and allow the roast to cool, in the broth for an additional 15 minutes.

Carefully remove the roast to a heatproof surface and allow it to cool completely.

Or, you can actually slice it while it's still warm and serve immediately.

We actually like to let it cool and then refrigerate it, to make slicing easier, then re-heat it later. We also find that the flavor matures if you let it sit in the fridge for several hours, or overnight.

REMEMBER - DON'T THROW AWAY THE BROTH.

Simply thickening the broth with a little cornstarch makes a nice gravy. You can also add additional spices, if you desire.

TIP: While this recipe is certainly easy to make by hand, we prefer to mix it in a stand mixer and do the kneading part with a dough hook. It comes out great!

SERVINGS: 14
CALORIES PER SERVING: 168
PROTEIN PER SERVING: 28.83 GRAMS

SOUPS

We love soups! They're so versatile. You can enjoy them for lunch or dinner. And, certainly, some of the soup recipes here are hearty enough for dinner.

CARROT & PUMPKIN SOUP

This is a smooth and tasty soup that evokes the flavors of autumn. Make it ahead to let the flavors mature. It also freezes well.

INGREDIENTS

4 tablespoons (60 ml) extra virgin olive oil

1 large yellow onion, chopped

1 tablespoon (15 ml) ginger root, peeled and finely diced

6 cloves garlic, minced

6 cups (1.5 L) vegetable broth

2 cups (475 ml) coconut milk

2 large carrots, peeled and chopped

4 cups (475 ml) pumpkin puree, or 1 - 30 oz. can

2 teaspoons (10 ml) pumpkin pie spice

1 teaspoon (5 ml) sea salt

½ teaspoon (2.5 ml) black pepper

DIRECTIONS

In a large pot, or dutch oven, heat the oil over medium heat.

When the oil is hot, add the onion, ginger and garlic and sauté for 5 minutes.

Add the broth, water, carrots and pumpkin and heat until it comes to a boil.

Reduce the heat and simmer, uncovered, until the carrots are very tender - about 30 minutes.

Purée the soup in batches using either a blender or a food processor.

Add the pumpkin spice and stir well.

Add the salt and pepper and stir again.

Serve immediately or cool and refrigerate or freeze for later use.

SERVINGS: 8
CALORIES PER SERVING: 243
PROTEIN PER SERVING: 3.09 GRAMS

Broccoli and Cauliflower Soup

$\mathcal{F}$eeling particularly hungry? Then this tasty soup, made in a slow cooker, may just be what you're looking for. There's lots and lots of veggies and this entire recipe can be considered only TWO servings, with each serving being LESS than 300 calories. You'll feel like you've had a huge meal and you can't beat all the nutrients packed into this vegan soup. As a bonus, the ingredients in this recipe are also great for detoxing.

INGREDIENTS

½ large yellow onion, chopped

½ large red onion, chopped

2 cups (350g) broccoli, cut in bite-size pieces

2 cups (650g) cauliflower, cut in bite-size pieces

2 cups (300g) carrots, chopped

4 red radishes, quartered

2 stalks celery, chopped

½ large rutabaga, peeled and chopped

2 cups (475 ml) vegetable broth, or water

1 key lime, thinly sliced including skin

1 inch (2.54 cm) fresh ginger, peeled and chopped

2 cloves garlic, chopped

1 teaspoon (5 ml) turmeric

1½ teaspoons (7.5 ml) rosemary

1½ teaspoons (7.5 ml) basil

1 cup (225g) baby spinach, packed

1 cup (67g) kale, thinly sliced, stalks removed

DIRECTIONS

Combine all of the ingredients, except the kale and spinach, in your slow cooker.

Set the slow cooker to low and cook for 7 to 8 hours.

20 minutes before the soup is done, turn the setting to high and add the spinach and kale.

Stir to mix them in and cook on high for 20 minutes.

Serve hot.

If there are any leftovers, this soup freezes well.

SERVINGS: 2 (BUT CERTAINLY ENOUGH FOR 4)

CALORIES PER SERVING (BASED ON 2 SERVINGS FOR THE ENTIRE RECIPE): 225

PROTEIN PER SERVING (BASED ON 2 SERVINGS FOR THE ENTIRE RECIPE): 9.57 GRAMS

Split Pea, Apple and Cabbage Soup

This soup is a particularly nice blend of complementary flavors. Be sure to use yellow split peas as their distinctive taste blends well with the apple and cabbage.

INGREDIENTS

2 teaspoons (10 ml) extra virgin olive oil

1 medium yellow onion, chopped

1 medium carrot, chopped

2 cloves garlic, minced

1 teaspoon (5 ml) fennel seed

1 cup (225g) split peas

5 cups (1.2 L) water or vegetable broth

½ small head cabbage, shredded

1 medium apple, chopped

1 teaspoon (5 ml) sea salt

1 teaspoon (5 ml) black pepper, freshly ground

DIRECTIONS

In a large saucepan, or medium Dutch oven, heat the olive oil.

Then add the onion, carrot, garlic and fennel seed.

Sauté for approximately 5 minutes.

Add the split peas and 5 cups (1.2 L) of water or broth. Stir well.

Bring to a boil, reduce heat and simmer, covered, for 1 hour.

Add the shredded cabbage and chopped apple, return the soup to a boil, reduce heat and simmer for 10 minutes.

Add the salt and pepper, stir well and serve.

SERVINGS: 4

CALORIES PER SERVING: 255

PROTEIN PER SERVING: 14.03 GRAMS

Red Cabbage and Carrot Soup

This soup is not only tasty, but great for detox and weight loss. You can actually eat as much as you like and feel very full on very few calories. That's right - all these ingredients amount to only two servings at only 228 calories/serving. Feel stuffed without feeling guilty!

INGREDIENTS

1 large yellow onion, large dice

2 large carrots, chopped

½ head red cabbage, cut in chunks

1 cup (110 g) bok choy, chopped

4 red radishes, quartered

2 large tomatoes, diced

6 sprigs parsley, chopped

2 stalks celery, chopped

1 medium summer squash, chopped

2 cups (475 ml) vegetable broth, or water

3 cloves garlic, minced

½ inch (1.25 cm) fresh ginger, peeled and minced

1 tablespoon (15 ml) soy sauce

1½ teaspoons (7.5 ml) dried rosemary

½ pound (226g) asparagus, cut in 2 inch pieces

DIRECTIONS

Place all of the ingredients in a slow cooker, with the exception of the asparagus, and cook on low for 8 hours.

30 minutes before the soup is done, add the asparagus and turn the slow cooker back up to high.

When the asparagus is soft, serve immediately.

SERVINGS: 2
CALORIES PER SERVING: 228
PROTEIN PER SERVING: 10.89 GRAMS

CABBAGE AND APPLE SOUP

Be sure to use unfiltered apple cider vinegar with "The Mother" for this recipe. It's not only good for you, it also aids in weight loss. You can use whatever kind of apple you like for this recipe. We often use Macintosh or Gala. It's okay to peel the apples, if that's what you prefer. We like to leave the skins on.

INGREDIENTS

1 cup (100g) green cabbage, shredded

1 cup (100g) red cabbage, shredded

1 large yellow onion, chopped

2 medium apples, cored and chopped

1 clove garlic, minced

1 teaspoon (5 ml) fresh ginger, grated

3 cups (700 ml) vegetable broth

½ cup (120 ml) unfiltered apple cider vinegar, with "The Mother"

¼ teaspoon (1.25 ml) cinnamon

½ teaspoon (2.5 ml) caraway seed

½ teaspoon (2.5 ml) black pepper, freshly ground

1 teaspoon (5 ml) sea salt

DIRECTIONS

Add all the ingredients to your slow cooker and stir well to combine.

Set the slow cooker on high for the first hour and then reduce to low.

Continue cooking on low for an additional 6-7 hours.

When the soup is ready, remove 1 cup (240 ml) and blend until smooth.

Return the blended soup to the slow cooker and stir well. This helps to thicken the soup.

Serve hot.

This soup freezes well.

SERVINGS: 4
CALORIES PER SERVING: 210
PROTEIN PER SERVING: 7.66 GRAMS

CORN AND CABBAGE CHOWDER

INGREDIENTS

3 cups (700 ml) vegetable broth, preferably homemade, divided

1 large russet potato, scrubbed and chopped

1 large yellow onion, chopped

4 cloves garlic, minced

1 teaspoon (5 ml) thyme

2 stalks celery, sliced

2 cups (200g) green cabbage, thinly sliced

1 cup (240 ml) coconut milk

1 cup (175g) frozen corn

1 teaspoon (5 ml) sea salt, or to taste

1 teaspoon (5 ml) black pepper, freshly ground, or to taste

1 tablespoon (15 ml) cornstarch, for thickening, if required

DIRECTIONS

In a large saucepan, heat about ¼ cup (60 ml) of the vegetable broth over medium heat.

Add the chopped potato, onion, celery, garlic and thyme and sauté for 3-4 minutes

Add the cabbage and sauté for another 1-2 minutes.

Add the rest of the vegetable broth and bring to a boil.

Reduce heat and simmer, uncovered for approximately 15 minutes.

Add the frozen corn and simmer for another 5 minutes.

Season with salt and freshly ground black pepper.

Add the coconut milk.

Note: if the soup needs thickening, combine the cornstarch with some of the coconut milk to make a pourable slurry. Slowly add the slurry to the simmering soup to achieve the consistency desired.

Serve immediately.

This recipe freezes well.

SERVINGS: 8
CALORIES PER SERVING: 134
PROTEIN PER SERVING: 2.8 GRAMS

DESSERTS

Yes, you can have desserts as a vegan - and - desserts other than just a piece of fruit!

CHIA SEED PUDDING

INGREDIENTS

1 cup plant-based milk of your choice

3 tablespoons Chia seeds (ground or whole)

¼ teaspoon vanilla

1 teaspoon Maple Syrup or sweetener of your choice (optional).

DIRECTIONS

Combine in a mason jar and shake until well mixed. Refrigerate for at least four hours. When ready, you can add any toppings you like - fruits, nuts, seeds, etc.

SERVINGS: 2
CALORIES PER SERVING: 145
PROTEIN PER SERVING: 3.95G

Piña Colada Nice Cream

An amazing dessert that is not only quick to make but vegan, too! While it packs a lot of taste, it doesn't come with anything except the 3 ingredients used – no refined sugar, no dairy, no preservatives and all taste!

INGREDIENTS

¼ cup coconut milk chilled

¼ cup pineapple chunks drained and frozen

1 large banana sliced and frozen

DIRECTIONS

Earlier in the day, prepare and freeze the pineapple chunks and banana slices and leave in freezer until ready to use.

In a small food processor, add the coconut milk first, then add the frozen pineapple and banana.

Process for about 1 minute until an ice cream consistency is reached.

Serve immediately.

See how to make it - https://blog.reluctantvegetarians.com/pina-colada-nice-cream-dessert/

SERVINGS: 1
CALORIES PER SERVING: 259
PROTEIN PER SERVING: 2.85G

TROPICAL DREAM SMOOTHIE

This super-creamy and wonderfully delicious and refreshing dessert smoothie can be made in the either alcoholic or non-alcoholic version.

You can use fresh pineapple as well, it should be juicy enough that you wouldn't have to add too much more liquid. If you do need more liquid, just add a little more coconut milk or some water.

INGREDIENTS

2 cups (475 ml) coconut milk

2 cups (450g) pineapple chunks, canned, including juice

1 large banana

4-6 ice cubes

4 ounces (120 ml) rum, optional

DIRECTIONS

Place all ingredients in the blender, with the exception of the rum.

Make sure the lid is secure and begin blending at lowest speed increasing gradually to maximum speed.

Blend for at least one minute or until everything is well blended and smooth.

Add the rum, if using, and blend for a few more seconds to get the rum well mixed in.

Serve immediately.

SERVINGS: 4

CALORIES PER SERVING (INCLUDING THE RUM): 372

PROTEIN PER SERVING: 3.11 GRAMS

Sugar-Free, Gluten-Free, Egg-Free, Oil-Free Strawberry Muffins

This recipe started as a way to eliminate sugar from a muffin recipe that we really liked and then evolved to cover a lot of scenarios that friends and family had been asking about. So we developed the recipe to also eliminate gluten, eggs and oil. The muffins are still wonderful and are also vegan.

INGREDIENTS

1 tablespoon (15 ml) ground flax seed

4 tablespoons (60 ml) water

⅔ cup (100g) sorghum flour

⅔ cup (100g) chickpea flour

1 cup (80g) gluten free quick oats

1 tablespoon (15 ml) baking powder

½ teaspoon (2.5 ml) sea salt

½ teaspoon (2.5 ml) cinnamon

1 cup (240 ml) rice milk, or plant milk of your choice

3 tablespoons (45 ml) unsweetened applesauce

1 teaspoon (5 ml) vanilla

1 cup (200g) strawberries, fresh or frozen, diced

DIRECTIONS

Pre-heat your oven to 350°F (180°C, Gas Mark 4) and grease a muffin tin (makes 12).

In a small bowl, combine the ground flax seed and water. Stir well and set aside. (This makes an egg substitute.)

In a large mixing bowl, combine the sorghum flour, chickpea flour, oats, baking powder, salt and cinnamon. Mix well.

In a separate bowl or measuring cup, combine the rice milk, applesauce, vanilla and flax seed mixture. Stir well.

Stir the liquid mixture into the dry mixture and mix just enough so that the dry ingredients are well moistened. Then fold in the diced strawberries.

Divide the batter evenly between the 12 muffin cups.

Bake at 350°F (180°C, Gas Mark 4) for 30-35 minutes or until a toothpick inserted in the center comes out clean and the muffins are slightly browned.

Remove the muffins from the oven and cool on a wire rack for about 10 minutes. Remove the muffins from the muffin tin and allow them to continue cooling on the wire rack.

Any leftover muffins will freeze well.

SERVINGS: 12
CALORIES PER SERVING: 88
PROTEIN PER SERVING: 2.85 GRAMS

Banana Cake

We always prefer to use glass baking dishes. We like to see how well the baked goods are browning. That gives us a good indication of whether or not they're actually done.

INGREDIENTS

1 tablespoon (15 ml) ground flax seed

4 tablespoons (60 ml) warm water

¼ cup (45g) brown sugar

1 teaspoon (5 ml) cinnamon

⅓ cup (80 ml) unsweetened applesauce

⅓ cup (80 ml) coconut milk

1 teaspoon (5 ml) vanilla extract

⅓ cup (80 ml) pure maple syrup

2 bananas, mashed

½ cup (65g) walnuts, chopped

1 cup (150g) whole wheat flour

1½ teaspoons (7.5 ml) baking powder

½ teaspoon (2.5 ml) sea salt

DIRECTIONS

Pre-heat the oven to 375°F (190°C, Gas Mark 5). Grease an 8-inch (20 cm) square baking dish.

In a small bowl, mix together the ground flax seed and warm water. Set aside to thicken.

In another small bowl, mix together the sugar and cinnamon. Set aside.

In a large mixing bowl, combine the applesauce, coconut milk, vanilla and maple syrup. Mix well. Then add the flax seed mixture and mix again. Add the chopped walnuts and mix again.

In a separate bowl or large measuring cup, mix together the flour, baking powder and salt. Mix well. Then add the flour mixture to the liquid mixture and stir until just combined. Do not over mix.

Pour the batter into the prepared baking dish and then sprinkle the sugar and cinnamon mixture evenly over the top of the batter.

Bake at 375°F (190°C, Gas Mark 5) for approximately 30 - 35 minutes, or until the center is set.

Remove from the oven and cool on a wire rack. Allow it to cool for several minutes before slicing.

SERVINGS: 12
CALORIES PER SERVING: 146
PROTEIN PER SERVING: 3.08 GRAMS

CONDIMENTS/SAUCES

A few extras to help "spice" up some of your meals.

Spicy Jalapeño Dill Hummus

We find that hummus is a great substitute for butter on a baked potato or on bread, in a sandwich.

INGREDIENTS

2 cups (330g) chickpeas, cooked

2 large kosher dill

2 tablespoons (30 ml) balsamic vinegar

¼ cup (60 ml) dill juice

¼ teaspoon (1.25 ml) salt

5 pickled jalapeño slices

DIRECTIONS

In this recipe we've used chickpeas that we cooked from dried. If you use canned chickpeas, be sure to drain and rinse them. Also, with canned chickpeas, you may need less liquid.

Place all of the ingredients in a food processor and blend until smooth.

SERVINGS: 24
CALORIES PER SERVING: 27
PROTEIN PER SERVING: 1.11 GRAMS

GEOFF'S FAMOUS HUMMUS

Geoff loves to experiment with hummus recipes and this is his "famous" recipe. Very, very tasty.

INGREDIENTS

1 can chickpeas, 15 ounces (443 ml), drained, reserve liquid

2 tablespoons (30 ml) sun dried tomatoes, not packed in water or oil

½ lime, juice only

3 cloves garlic

6 slices jalapeño, or to taste

1 tablespoon (15 ml) tahini paste

½ teaspoon (2.5 ml) sea salt

½ teaspoon (1.25 ml) freshly ground black pepper

1 tablespoon (15 ml) balsamic vinegar

DIRECTIONS

Place all ingredients, in order listed, in a food processor and blend until smooth.

Add reserved liquid as required to achieve desired consistency. You'll probably need about half of the liquid.

SERVINGS: 24

CALORIES PER SERVING: 18

PROTEIN PER SERVING: 0.84 GRAMS

Vegan Spaghetti Sauce

We had such a large crop of tomatoes in our garden that we froze lots of them. We just washed them, cored them and froze them. This recipe is based on using frozen tomatoes, but you could just as easily use very ripe fresh tomatoes (organic, of course) if you prefer.

INGREDIENTS

5 cups (1 Kg) whole frozen tomatoes, thawed and puréed (about 12)

1 yellow onion, chopped

1 tablespoon (15 ml) garlic, chopped

⅓ cup (20 g) sun dried tomatoes, chopped

1 tablespoon (15 ml) Italian seasoning

¼ teaspoon (1.25 ml) red pepper flakes

1 tablespoon (15 ml) sea salt

6 ounces (180 ml) tomato paste

DIRECTIONS

Allow the whole frozen tomatoes to thaw overnight in a colander, to let the excess water drip off.

Purée the tomatoes, skins and all, in a blender. It should make about 5-6 cups (1 Kg).

Add the puréed tomatoes to the slow cooker, then add the rest of the ingredients and stir well.

Set the slow cooker to low and cook for 8-10 hours, stirring occasionally .

SERVINGS: 8
CALORIES PER SERVING: 70
PROTEIN PER SERVING: 3.51 GRAMS

Sugar-Free Stir Fry Sauce

In this recipe the dates, as well as the red pepper flakes are optional. The dates, however, almost double the calorie count of this sauce. In addition to that there is, naturally, fructose in the dates and because the sauce is being blended smooth, a lot of the effect of the fiber in the dates is diminished. But don't panic, all the fiber in the vegetables that go into the stir fry will offset any negative effect from the fructose

INGREDIENTS

2 cups (475 ml) vegetable broth

¼ cup (60 ml) soy sauce

3 tablespoons (45 ml) cornstarch

1 inch (2.54 cm) fresh ginger, piece, minced

4 cloves garlic, minced

2 Medjool dates, chopped

¼ teaspoon (1.25 ml) red pepper flakes, optional

DIRECTIONS

Combine all ingredients in a food processor and blend until smooth.

Add to stir fry recipes as instructed.

SERVINGS: 4
CALORIES PER SERVING WITH DATES: 74
CALORIES PER SERVING WITHOUT DATES: 41
PROTEIN PER SERVING WITH DATES: 1.74G
PROTEIN PER SERVING WITHOUT DATES: 1.53G

TRADITIONAL STIR FRY SAUCE

INGREDIENTS

½ cup (60g) cornstarch

¼ cup (45g) brown sugar, packed

1 teaspoon (5 ml) ground ginger

2 cloves garlic, minced

½ teaspoon (2.5 ml) chili powder

½ cup (120 ml) soy sauce

¼ cup (60 ml) apple cider vinegar

2 cups (475 ml) vegetable broth

½ cup (120 ml) water

DIRECTIONS

Place all of the ingredients in a blender and blend until well mixed. Use immediately or refrigerate or freeze for later use.

SERVINGS: 4
CALORIES PER SERVING: 142
PROTEIN PER SERVING: 2.83G

SALAD DRESSINGS

Nice additions to your favorite salads.

SPICY TAHINI DRESSING

INGREDIENTS

½ cup (120 ml) tahini paste

¾ cup (180 ml) water

4 tablespoons (60 ml) lemon juice

1 clove garlic, finely minced

Salt and pepper to taste

1 tablespoon (15 ml) Sriracha

DIRECTIONS

Combine all ingredients in a blender and blend until well mixed.

SERVINGS: 16
CALORIES PER SERVING: 46
PROTEIN PER SERVING: 1.34 GRAMS

Spicy Chipotle Dressing

INGREDIENTS

½ cup (120 ml) unsweetened almond milk (or other non-dairy milk)

4 teaspoons (20 ml) ground flaxseed

2 tablespoons (30 ml) lemon juice

1 tablespoon (15 ml) apple cider vinegar

1 Medjool date, pitted

1 small clove garlic

1 teaspoon (5 ml) salt, or to taste

2 teaspoons (10 ml) tomato paste

½ teaspoon (2.5 ml) chipotle chili powder, or to taste

½ teaspoon (2.5 ml) ground cumin

additional milk or water as needed

DIRECTIONS

Place all ingredients in a blender and blend on high speed until smooth.

Don't worry if it seems a bit thin, it will thicken when you refrigerate it.

Pour the dressing into a jar and refrigerate to thicken and allow the flavors to develop.

If the dressing becomes too thick, you can thin it with some additional almond milk or water.

SERVINGS: 6
CALORIES PER SERVING: 28
PROTEIN PER SERVING: 0.61 GRAMS

BONUS RECIPES

A few extra recipes to help you along in your vegan journey.

SUPER QUICK AND EASY MEALS

We all have those days! Days when we are hurried, tired, stressed, all of the above and we don't want to have to do too much to get dinner on the table.

We like to keep quick items in the freezer for days like this.

Here's a few quick recipes to help you stay on track on busy days.

ITALIAN SAUSAGES AND PEPPERS

A classic dish redefined.

This recipe uses store-bought vegan sausages, so it's quick, easy, healthy AND vegan!

This dish can be served with a pasta and veggies or with potatoes or with a salad. It's your choice!

We like to make this on those nights when we don't feel like making more complicated recipes.

INGREDIENTS

4 Vegan sausages, Italian flavor, sliced

1 large yellow onion, halved and sliced

2 medium red bell pepper, sliced

2 cups (475 ml) tomato sauce

1 tablespoon (15 ml) garlic, minced

1 tablespoon (15 ml) fresh basil, chopped

DIRECTIONS

In a large regular, or cast iron, skillet sauté the onions in a little water (or vegetable broth) until translucent.

Add the sliced peppers and sauté for another minute or two.

Add the tomato sauce, garlic and basil.

Add the sliced sausage.

Bring to a simmer over medium heat and simmer for 5 minutes to make sure that the sausage is heated through.

Serve immediately.

SERVINGS: 4
CALORIES PER SERVING: 181
PROTEIN PER SERVING: 13.72 GRAMS

Veggie Sausages Baked in Sauerkraut

We love sauerkraut and this recipe couldn't be easier. We've made it with frozen sausages and it came out great. Just serve it with veggies of your choice. We generally throw a couple of potatoes in the oven and bake them at the same time we're cooking the sausages and then just microwave some frozen corn or peas. Easy peasy!

INGREDIENTS

4 vegan sausages (we used Field Roast® sausages - frozen)

2 cups (475 ml) sauerkraut

DIRECTIONS

Preheat the oven to 425°F (220°C, Gas Mark 7).

Coat a glass loaf pan with non-stick cooking spray.

Add the frozen sausages to the loaf pan and cover them with the sauerkraut.

Cover the dish with foil and place in the oven.

Bake for 40 minutes at 425°F (220°C, Gas Mark 7).

When cooking time is up, remove the dish from the oven and place on a heatproof surface.

Carefully remove the foil.

Serve the sausages and sauerkraut with the veggies of your choice.

SERVINGS: 4
CALORIES PER SERVING: 205
PROTEIN PER SERVING: 16.0 GRAMS

BONUS RECIPES FOR THE INSTANT POT®

Many of us are now taking advantage of the Instant Pot® (or other electric pressure cookers) to make tasty, nutritious vegan meals. Here's a few recipes we developed for the Instant Pot®.

Note: In some of these recipes we have attempted to give you the "complete" cooking time. That means the time to come to pressure, the cooking time, the pressure release time (be that a Quick or Natural Pressure release).

Sorry, but not all the recipes have that. Even though we have made all of these dishes ourselves, we haven't always remembered to record all of the times.

Detox Cabbage Stew

This recipe is not only easy - just dump everything in your Instant Pot® and stir - it is also oil-free and very, very low calorie.

This makes approximately 10 servings and each serving weighs in at only 185 calories!

We made this recipe in an 8-quart Instant Pot®, but it should work just fine in a 6-quart, too.

INGREDIENTS

½ large cabbage, quartered and sliced

1 large yellow onion, quartered and sliced

2 stalks celery, chopped

3 large carrots, chopped

8 medium radishes, halved or quartered, depending on size

1 cup (36g) baby Swiss chard, optional

28 ounces (796 ml) diced tomatoes

1 tablespoon (15 ml) garlic, minced

3 tablespoons (45 ml) apple cider vinegar

1½ tablespoons (22.5 ml) lemon juice

1 teaspoon (5 ml) sea salt

1 teaspoon (5 ml) black pepper, freshly ground

3 teaspoons (15 ml) Herbes de Provence or Italian seasoning

½ teaspoon (2.5 ml) red pepper flakes, optional

1½ cups (245g) chickpeas, canned and drained or home cooked

4 cups (975 ml) vegetable broth

DIRECTIONS

Prepare all of the ingredients per the ingredient list.

Add all ingredients to the inner pot of your Instant Pot® and give it a good stir.

Close and lock the lid, ensuring the Pressure Valve is in the Sealing position.

Select the Soup/Broth mode and set the cooking time for 5 minutes. (Be patient - it can take up to 30 minutes for the pot to come to pressure and seal before counting down the cooking time)

Once the cooking time is complete, allow a 10 minute NPR (Natural Pressure Release).

Hint: allowing a 10 minute NPR allows the contents to "settle down" a bit before you release the pressure, so you're less likely to get anything spewing out of the Pressure Valve.

When the 10 minutes is up, release the rest of the pressure by carefully turning the Pressure Valve from Sealing to Venting.

When all of the pressure is released and the Float Valve has dropped, carefully remove the lid.

Carefully remove the inner liner to a heatproof surface, give the stew a good stir and serve immediately.

Note: This stew freezes well, so you can freeze any leftovers to use later.

SERVINGS: 10
CALORIES PER SERVING: 185
PROTEIN PER SERVING: 9.3 GRAMS

Eggplant and Sweet Potato Curry

INGREDIENTS

¾ cup (150g) green lentils

2 cups (475 ml) vegetable broth, preferably homemade

1 medium yellow onion, chopped

4 cloves garlic, minced

1 tablespoon (15 ml) ginger, minced

½ teaspoon (2.5 ml) turmeric

1 tablespoon (15 ml) curry powder

1 teaspoon (5 ml) cumin

28 ounces (796 ml) diced tomatoes, canned

4 cups (1000g) eggplant, chopped

4 cups (600g) sweet potato, chopped

1 teaspoon (5 ml) sea salt

2 cups (450g) baby spinach, washed and packed

½ cup (120 ml) coconut milk

DIRECTIONS

Prepare all the ingredients per the list of ingredients.

Add all the ingredients to the inner pot of the Instant Pot®, with the exception of the spinach and the coconut milk.

Close and lock the lid, ensuring that the Pressure Valve is in the Sealing Position.

Select the Pressure Cook (or Manual) button and set the cooking time for 4 minutes.

Once the cooking time is complete, allow a 10 minute Natural Pressure Release, then carefully turn the Pressure Valve from Sealing to Venting to release any remaining pressure.

Once all the pressure has been released and the Float Valve has dropped, carefully remove the lid. Then, carefully remove the inner pot to a heatproof surface.

Add the spinach and coconut milk. Stir well and serve with rice and/or your favorite side dishes.

This recipe freezes well if you want to freeze any leftovers.

SERVINGS: 8
CALORIES PER SERVING: 239
PROTEIN PER SERVING: 8.59 GRAMS
TOTAL TIME: 47 TO 60 MINUTES, BASED ON THE FOLLOWING:
PREP TIME: 10-15 MINUTES
TIME TO COME TO PRESSURE: 18-23 MINUTES
TIME AT PRESSURE: 4 MINUTES
NATURAL PRESSURE RELEASE (NPR): 10 MINUTES
TIME FOR PRESSURE TO RELEASE COMPLETELY: 5-8 MINUTES

Red Lentil & Mushroom Pasta Sauce

Although this recipe is for 6 servings, we find it often goes much further than that.

So, at only 311 calorie per serving, if you stretch it further, then that, naturally, reduces the calories/serving.

This recipe is also oil-free!

IMPORTANT NOTE:

DO NOT STIR, AND MAKE SURE THE BROTH IS ON THE BOTTOM. IF THE TOMATOES ARE IN CONTACT WITH THE BOTTOM YOU COULD GET A "BURN NOTICE" ON YOUR INSTANT POT®. WE KNOW THIS FROM EXPERIENCE.

INGREDIENTS

4 cups (950 ml) vegetable broth

1½ (300g) cups red lentils, rinsed

1 large yellow onion, diced

2 stalks celery, diced

3 medium carrots, diced

12 ounces (340g) Cremini mushrooms, quartered

4 cloves garlic, diced

28 ounces (796 ml) crushed tomatoes, canned

28 ounces (796 ml) diced tomatoes, canned

3 tablespoons (45 ml) tomato paste

1½ teaspoons (7.5 ml) sea salt

2 teaspoons (10 ml) thyme

2 teaspoons (10 ml) oregano

1 teaspoon (5 ml) basil

¼ teaspoon (1.25 ml) red pepper flakes

DIRECTIONS

Prepare all the ingredients per the list of ingredients.

Add all the ingredients to the inner pot of the Instant Pot®.

Close and lock the lid of the Instant Pot®, ensuring that the Pressure Valve is in the Sealing Position.

Select the Pressure Cook (or Manual) button and set the cooking time for 2 minutes.

Once the cooking time is complete, allow a 5 minute Natural Pressure Release, then carefully turn the Pressure Valve from Sealing to Venting to release any remaining pressure.

Once all the pressure has been released and the Float Valve has dropped, carefully remove the lid. Then, carefully remove the inner pot to a heatproof surface.

Stir well and serve immediately over your favorite pasta or rice.

Note: This pasta sauce freezes well.

CREMINI POT ROAST

Who says a pot roast has to include meat? This recipe features hearty Cremini (baby bella) mushrooms as the basis for this healthy pot roast.

This recipe is also oil-free!

Serve with a side-dish of your choice, some crusty bread and, of course, your favorite wine.

Note: When we tested this recipe, it took approximately 18 minutes to come to pressure in a 6-quart Instant Pot®.

INGREDIENTS

4 medium red potatoes, chunked

1 pound (454g) Cremini mushrooms, halved

4 medium carrots, chunked

2 large parsnips, chunked

1 large yellow onion, sliced

4 cloves garlic, minced

2 teaspoons (10 ml) thyme

3 cups (700 ml) vegetable broth, divided

½ cup (120 ml) dry red wine

3 tablespoons (45 ml) tomato paste

2 tablespoons (30 ml) vegan Worcestershire sauce

Add the following after Pot Roast is cooked to thicken the gravy:

2 tablespoons (30 ml) cornstarch

sea salt, to taste

black pepper, freshly ground, to taste

DIRECTIONS

Prepare all the ingredients per the list of ingredients.

Add all the ingredients to the inner pot of the Instant Pot®, reserving a couple of tablespoons of the vegetable broth to mix with the cornstarch later.

Close and lock the lid, ensuring that the Pressure Valve is in the Sealing Position.

Select the Pressure Cook (or Manual) button and set the cooking time for 2 minutes.

Once the cooking time is complete, allow a 4 minute Natural Pressure Release, then carefully turn the Pressure Valve from Sealing to Venting to release any remaining pressure.

Once the pressure has been released and the Float Valve has dropped, carefully remove the lid, and switch to Sauté mode.

Mix the cornstarch with 2 tablespoons of vegetable broth to make a pourable slurry.

With the contents still bubbling, slowly pour in the cornstarch slurry, stirring constantly until the gravy has thickened. Add salt and pepper to taste.

Serve immediately with your favorite side dish(es).

Note: This recipe freezes well.

SERVINGS: 4

CALORIES PER SERVING: 338

PROTEIN PER SERVING: 9.38 GRAMS

Detox Vegetable and Red Lentil Soup

It's always nice when something that's good for you is also delicious. This soup certainly is both! And, not only that but the ingredients aid in detox and weight loss, too!

Note: When we tested this recipe, it took approximately 28 minutes to come to pressure in an 8-quart Instant Pot®. After the 10 minute Natural Pressure Release, when we turned the Pressure Valve to Venting, it took approximately 3 minutes for the rest of the pressure to release and the Float Valve to drop.

INGREDIENTS

1 cup (200g) red lentils

1 large yellow onion, diced

4 cloves garlic, minced

1 inch (2.54 cm) ginger, piece, minced

4 stalks celery, sliced

2 cups (350g) broccoli, florets, chopped

1 cup (325g) cauliflower, florets, chopped

28 ounces (796 ml) canned tomatoes, diced

2 teaspoons (10 ml) turmeric

2 teaspoons (10 ml) chili powder

1½ teaspoons (7.5 ml) sea salt

1 teaspoon (5 ml) black pepper, freshly ground

6 cups (1.5 L) vegetable broth, preferably homemade

DIRECTIONS

We used an 8-quart (8 L) Instant Pot® for this recipe but it will work just as well in a 6-quart (6 L).

Prepare all the ingredients per the list of ingredients.

Add all the ingredients to the inner pot of the Instant Pot®.

Close and lock the lid, ensuring that the Pressure Valve is in the Sealing Position.

Select the Soup/Broth button and set the cooking time for 5 minutes.

Once the cooking time is complete, allow a 10 minute Natural Pressure Release, then carefully turn the Pressure Valve from Sealing to Venting to release any remaining pressure.

Once all the pressure has been released and the Float Valve has dropped, carefully remove the lid.

Then, carefully remove the inner pot to a heatproof surface.

Stir well and serve immediately.

This soup also freezes well.

SERVINGS: 8
CALORIES PER SERVING: 141
PROTEIN PER SERVING: 8.37 GRAMS

WHITE BEAN & BEET GREENS SOUP

We certainly hope that, when you purchase (or grow) beets, that you don't throw out the greens (tops). They are not only edible but they are delicious and extremely good for you.

We frequently get a bumper crop of beets from our garden so we usually have lots of both beets and beet greens in the freezer through the winter. Frozen beet greens can go right into the Instant Pot® still frozen. And, we've found, that the greens are pretty easy to chop while they're frozen.

INGREDIENTS

1 medium yellow onion, chopped

2 medium carrots, chopped

2 stalks celery, chopped

4 cloves garlic, minced

1 teaspoon (5 ml) rosemary

1 teaspoon (5 ml) thyme

1 teaspoon (5 ml) poultry seasoning

1 teaspoon (5 ml) red pepper flakes

2 tablespoons (30 ml) white vinegar

1 tablespoon (15 ml) soy sauce

6 cups (1.5 L) vegetable broth, preferably homemade

2 cups (400g) white beans, soaked overnight

2 large tomatoes, chopped

3 cups (114g) beet greens, chopped

1 teaspoon (5 ml) Himalayan pink salt or sea salt

1 teaspoon (5 ml) black pepper, freshly ground

DIRECTIONS

We used a 6-quart (6 L) Instant Pot® for this recipe but it will work just as well in a 8-quart (8 L).

Prepare all the ingredients per the list of ingredients.

Add all the ingredients to the inner pot of the Instant Pot®.

Close and lock the lid, ensuring that the Pressure Valve is in the Sealing Position.

Select the Soup/Broth button and set the cooking time for 15 minutes.

Once the cooking time is complete, allow a 10 minute Natural Pressure Release, then carefully turn the Pressure Valve from Sealing to Venting to release any remaining pressure.

Once all the pressure has been released and the Float Valve has dropped, carefully remove the lid.

Then, carefully remove the inner pot to a heatproof surface.

Stir well and serve immediately or freeze for later.

SERVINGS: 10

CALORIES PER SERVING: 172

PROTEIN PER SERVING: 10.46 GRAMS

SOME ADDITIONAL USEFUL INFO

TOTAL TIME: 64 - 70 MINUTES, BASED ON THE FOLLOWING:

PREP TIME: 10-15 MINUTES

TIME TO COME TO PRESSURE: 25 MINUTES

TIME AT PRESSURE: 15 MINUTES

NATURAL PRESSURE RELEASE (NPR): 10 MINUTES

TIME FOR PRESSURE TO RELEASE COMPLETELY: 4 MINUTES

Instant Pot® Mulligatawny Soup

Mulligatawny sounds like it should be Irish but then you discover it contains curry so now you think it's Indian. Well that's sort of right but mulligatawny is actually an English soup based on a Tamil recipe. Look it up on Wikipedia.

This soup is frequently made with chicken but this is the vegan version.

INGREDIENTS

1 tablespoon (15 mL) extra virgin olive oil

2 carrots, peeled and roughly chopped

2 onions, roughly chopped

1 stalk of celery, roughly chopped

3 slices of fresh ginger (about quarter size) peeled

5 cloves of garlic, roughly chopped

2 tablespoons (30 mL) curry powder

1 teaspoon (5 mL) ground coriander

6 cups (1.4 L) vegetable broth, homemade if possible

1 medium baking potato, scrubbed but unpeeled, roughly chopped

¾ cup (180 mL) coconut milk

2 tablespoons (30 mL) lime juice, fresh if possible

3 tablespoons (3g) fresh cilantro, chopped (optional)

DIRECTIONS

Select the Sauté mode and allow the inner liner to heat up slightly.

Add the olive oil, carrots, onions, celery, ginger and garlic and sauté for 2-3 minutes.

Add the curry and coriander and sauté for another minute.

Add the vegetable broth and stir, using a wooden or silicone spatula to scrape any bits off the bottom of the pot.

Add the chopped potato and stir.

Turn off Sauté mode.

Close and lock the lid of the Instant Pot® ensuring the Pressure Valve is in the Sealing position.

Select the Soup/Broth mode and set the cooking time for 18 minutes.

Once cooking time is complete, allow a Natural Pressure Release for 10 minutes and then manually release the rest of the pressure.

When all of the pressure has been released and the Float Valve has dropped, unlock and remove the lid.

Carefully remove the inner liner to a heatproof surface.

Using an immersion blender, blend the soup until smooth, then add the coconut milk and lime juice and stir well.

Serve immediately, using the chopped cilantro as a garnish, if desired.

This soup also freezes well.

SERVINGS: 6
CALORIES PER SERVING: 177
PROTEIN PER SERVING: 3.17 GRAMS

Easy Instant Pot® Minestrone Soup

$\mathcal{P}$ositively packed with protein, this soup is hearty enough to serve as a meal with some crusty bread on the side. This Instant Pot® version is easy to make and you can freeze any leftovers for later use.

INGREDIENTS

7 cups (1.65 L) vegetable broth, preferably home made

1½ cups (150g) pasta, your choice (we used macaroni)

1 medium yellow onion, chopped

2 large carrots, chopped

1 stalk celery, sliced

1 medium zucchini, chopped

4 cloves garlic, minced

3½ cups (796 ml) diced tomatoes, approximately a 28-ounce can

1½ cups (90g) kidney beans, or beans of your choice, canned or home cooked (we've also used black beans in this recipe)

1½ teaspoons (7.5 ml) oregano

1½ teaspoons (7.5 ml) rosemary

1 teaspoon (5 ml) tarragon

1 teaspoon (5 ml) thyme

1 teaspoon (5 ml) sea salt

1 teaspoon (5 ml) pepper, freshly ground

2 cups (450g) baby spinach or beet greens

DIRECTIONS

Add all of the ingredients to the inner liner of your Instant Pot® in the order given, making sure the pasta is completely covered by the liquid.

DO NOT STIR. This is because you want the other ingredients to hold the pasta under the liquid so it cooks properly.

Close and lock the lid, ensuring that the Pressure Valve is in the Sealing position.

Select the Soup/Broth mode and set the cooking time for 4 minutes.

Once the cooking time is complete, allow a 5 minute Natural Pressure Release (this allows the contents to "settle down" a bit before you release the pressure).

Then, release the remaining pressure by carefully turning the Pressure Valve from Sealing to Venting.

When all the pressure has been released, carefully remove the lid and then transfer the inner pot to a heatproof surface.

Give the soup and good stir and serve immediately.

Note: this soup freezes well.

SERVINGS: 12
CALORIES PER SERVING: 403
PROTEIN PER SERVING: 18.32 GRAMS

JUST ONE MORE THING

- Did you enjoy reading this book?
- Do you think you got good value?
- Did it deliver what we promised in the description?

If you answered no to any of the questions above please return this book for a full refund. If you answered yes, please leave a review so that others will feel confident buying their own copy of this book.

Reviews are incredibly important to independent authors so we sincerely hope you will do us the courtesy of leaving a review for your fellow Reluctant Vegetarians.

We know you are busy and it will take a little bit of your time to leave the review so it's only fair we offer a small gift in return. The truth is you can get the gift if you leave a review or not, but we hope you do.

Just go to the URL below to claim it.

Thank you,

Geoff and Vicky Wells

Your reward is waiting for you at:

https://fun.reluctantvegetarians.com/veganreward

UNANNOUNCED BONUS

We write a lot of books and we hope you will always be happy with your purchases from us.

"Under promise and over deliver," has always been a motto of ours, so to thank you for your purchase we would like to give you a free bonus.

Just go to -

https://fun.reluctantvegetarians.com/veganbonus

to claim it.

OTHER BOOKS IN THE RELUCTANT VEGETARIAN SERIES

This is the fifth book in the Reluctant Vegetarian series. The other four are available from Amazon in print, ebook, large print and audio editions.

Many of our books have been translated into Spanish, French Italian, Portuguese, Afrikaans and Japanese.

Check out any of these books by going to:

https://geezerguides.com